Praise for *Warfare Praying*

When I was serving The Moody Church in Chicago, I met regularly for prayer with my friend Mark Bubeck, and I can assure you that he knows the ins and outs of the prayer life. If warfare prayer is new to you, this book will both instruct you and motivate you to move into the "victory army." If you have been a dedicated "prayer warrior" for years, this book will still enlighten you and encourage you. This new edition of a masterful study is just what the church needs today.

Warren W. Wiersbe
Author, pastor, Bible teacher, and conference speaker

When I think of a prayer warrior the first name that comes to mind is Mark Bubeck. He has modeled everything taught in this book and been a source of encouragement and guidance to thousands throughout his ministry. I am honored to have worked with him and learned from him for over a decade and know you will be helped in practical and life-giving ways by the material in this book.

Marcus Warner
President, Deeper Walk International, and coauthor of
Rare Leadership

Reading this book will transform your prayer life and affect every area of your life. Don't read it if you don't want to change and want to drift along with your lesser pattern of praying. Do read it if you want to make a significant quality difference in your life, your church life, and in your society for the gospel of Christ and the glory of God.

C. Fred Dickason
Professor Emeritus, Moody Bible Institute

Having read many books regarding our Adversary, I have often been disappointed. They often seemed a bit unbalanced and overly focused on seeing a demon behind every problem. Mark's book is different. It is extremely balanced, very practical, and delightfully authentic. Illustrations from his own experience in the battle with the enemy permeate the whole book. Most important to me is the thoughtful and accurate weaving together of a large number of biblical passages that are often neglected. Mark has put me on alert and given me new insight on how to pray against the enemy of our souls.

JOSEPH DILLOW
Founder of Biblical Education by Extension World (BEE), and author of *The Reign of the Servant Kings* and *Final Destiny*

Through this book written years ago, and now refreshed, are reflections straight from the old warrior's heart. Every Christian needs to read this book!

LINDA DILLOW
Author of *Calm My Anxious Heart*, and coauthor of *Surprised by the Healer* and *Passion Pursuit*

This is a book that should be read by every thoughtful Christian. Mark Bubeck not only exposes the work and strategy of our enemy Satan, but also teaches us how we can overcome him by participating in the victory Jesus Christ wrought on our behalf. This book will build your faith. It will give you the insight and confidence you need to confront our defeated foe. Yes, we are in a war, but we have resources to fight from the standpoint of victory. Read this book carefully, read it often, and share what you have learned with a friend.

DR. ERWIN W. LUTZER
Pastor Emeritus, The Moody Church

WARFARE PRAYING

BIBLICAL STRATEGIES FOR OVERCOMING THE ADVERSARY

MARK I. BUBECK

MOODY PUBLISHERS

CHICAGO

Edited by Judy Dunagan and Kevin Emmert
Interior design: Ragont Design
Cover design: Design Corps

Library of Congress Cataloging-in-Publication Data

Names: Bubeck, Mark I., author.
Title: Warfare praying : biblical strategies for overcoming the adversary / Mark I. Bubeck.
Description: Chicago : Moody Publishers, 2016. | Description based on print version record and CIP data provided by publisher; resource not viewed.
Identifiers: LCCN 2016020383 (print) | LCCN 2016019856 (ebook) | ISBN 9780802494153 () | ISBN 9780802414533
Subjects: LCSH: Spiritual warfare. | Prayer--Christianity. | Devil--Christianity. | Demonology.
Classification: LCC BV4509.5 (print) | LCC BV4509.5 .B8234 2016 (ebook) | DDC 235/.4--dc23
LC record available at https://lccn.loc.gov/2016020383

Moody Publishers
820 N. La Salle Boulevard
Chicago, IL 60610

1 3 5 7 9 10 8 6 4 2

Printed in the United States of America

This book is dedicated to the cherished memory of my beloved wife, Anita Bubeck (November 19, 1928–January 8, 2013)

"No one ever had a wife who loved her husband more than Anita loved me." Such words have been spoken from my lips and grateful heart a multitude of times. Those are not just romantic memories or my emotional feelings. They express what my dear wife communicated by her life and actions in a multitude of ways.

Although I miss her presence, her steadfast love still refreshes and encourages me on a daily basis.

The message of this book is one she loved and lived as she walked so faithfully by my side.

May the Truth of God's Word fortify the life and ministry of every believer who reads this book!

CONTENTS

PART III—THE WHOLE ARMOR OF GOD

A WORD FROM THE AUTHOR

Holy. Infinite. Eternal. Omnipotent. Almighty. These are "God" words. They belong to Him alone and express truth about Him that will stand forever. This truth will never change. The Bible shares God's truth with us. His Word is an anchor for understanding divine, eternal truth. Oh what a treasure God has given us through His Word!

The devil is a liar. He is the great deceiver. Everything he does and stands for is meant to advance and promote his lies. Truth defeats and devastates the devil's schemes and plans.

This book, formerly titled *Overcoming the Adversary,* is meant to be a helpful tool to assist believers in verbalizing truth in prayer. Focusing God's truth on present-day needs remains one of the major goals of all prayer.

As I have been working on this update of the book that was published more than thirty years ago, I have been amazed by the contemporary relevance of its message. It has refreshed and renewed my own appreciation of what God has placed in our hands by His divine revelation, His beloved Word.

I just had a birthday. I am now eighty-eight years of age. God has taught me to use doctrinal prayer, which is biblical truth applied in prayer, over my family and for our troubled world for many years. I am more convinced than ever that God's truth always wins! It never fails. We are always on the side of victory when we are able to focus the truth on every situation of life.

The experiences that come to us through the passing of time

are an important element or factor in God's teaching process. The personal profit that I've experienced in working on this update of the book is measureless. My prayer is that those who read and study its message will experience similar spiritual uplift.

May God use the message of this book to help His people continue growing and learning how to use doctrinal prayer. And may God help His people walk in the victory He has provided for them.

That is my prayer for His people.

MARK I. BUBECK

INTRODUCTION

I keep my eyes always on the LORD. *With him at my right hand, I will not be shaken.* (Psalm 16:8)

Cast your cares on the LORD *and he will sustain you; he will never let the righteous be shaken.* (Psalm 55:22)

I can do all this through him who gives me strength. (Philippians 4:13)

B oth the Old and New Testaments convey to us that there is a secure, immovable, invincible place of victory for God's people. It is God's plan that those who belong to Christ will always be able to do God's will. No enemy can interfere with that plan unless believers allow that enemy to rob them of their victorious stance. The purpose of this book is to help believers grasp a prayer practice that will enable them to walk in victory.

The reader will find occasional references to my book *The Adversary,* the prequel to this book. It was written in response to many requests for an additional, practical "handbook" on spiritual warfare.

The emphasis of this book is prayer, a discipline that is often disgracefully neglected among evangelical Christians. One report has indicated that even "the average pastor surveyed prays only three minutes each day."[1] Sadly, though that statistic dates back to 1979, I think it still holds true today. If that presents even a partial picture of what is happening in the prayer life of the church, we are in serious trouble.

The following call of Andrew Murray needs to be heeded today:

> A most important phase of prayer is intercession. What a work God has set open for those who are His priests-intercessors! We find a wonderful expression in the prophecy of Isaiah; God says, "Let him take hold of me;" and again, "There is none that stirreth up himself to take hold of thee." In other passages God refers to the intercessors for Israel. Have you ever taken hold of God? The church and the world need nothing so much as a mighty Spirit of intercession to bring down the power of God on earth. Pray for the descent from heaven of the Spirit of intercession for a great prayer revival.[2]

When I first wrote this book in 1984, I fervently desired that it would awaken the reader to the awesome resource and power of prayer. Now more than thirty years later, that heart's cry is even more acute.

Not a Passing Fad

As she came into my office, her eyes brimmed with tears, and her countenance betrayed her anxiety. Her voice had the same quiver of fear I had noted when she had called for an appointment. Nancy[3] was the daughter of missionaries, a brilliant student, and a beautiful nineteen-year-old.

After a few moments of prayer, she opened her heart. "Pastor Bubeck, I've been tormented for several months now. Almost every night when I try to sleep, the sense of a fearful presence seems to close in on me. I've even seen ghostlike apparitions in my room, and I'm so afraid."

Nancy's problem had started when she and some of her classmates at a Christian college had seen the film *The Exorcist*. Since that time her torments had come with varying intensity.

She wanted to know where she could find help. How could she be free from this fear? Was her anxiety purely psychological—was she losing her mind? Or could it be that Satan or his demons were causing her problem? If so, what could she do?

I showed Nancy some of the principles for spiritual warfare set forth in the Word of God. New insights, and with them renewed confidence, began to build in her heart. As she saw her victory in the Lord Jesus Christ, some of the fear began to drain away.

Nancy's problem is a growing one in the church today. Before she left my office she asked a question that deserves an answer. "I'm seeing a whole new side to the Christian life that I've never seen before. Why is it that in the nineteen years of my life I've scarcely heard about spiritual warfare?" I thought I detected a note of resentment, as though she felt cheated as a Christian.

A number of believers want an answer to that question. Why all of this renewed interest in Christian circles concerning demons and Satan's work? Is it just another passing fad? Does it center too much attention on the devil? Is it a subtle attempt of Satan to turn believers away from the important work of evangelism?

Satan's work certainly is not a passing fad. He has always hated all believers with a "cruel hatred," the kind described in Psalm 25:19 (kjv). Satan's kingdom is engaged in a relentless effort to destroy Christians and their effective fulfillment of God's will. There are several reasons the battle is becoming more open today.

One reason for increased overt activity of Satan in the lives of Christians is that often the subject of aggressive spiritual warfare has been largely neglected in evangelical circles. Believers in America have been lulled into an attitude of passively assuming their victory over Satan instead of aggressively applying it. When the Lord first led me into a deeper study of how the believer defeats Satan's power, I discovered that most of the sound doctrinal books written on the subject were very old. Evangelical seminaries and Bible schools have prepared their graduates to battle for the fundamentals of the faith but have provided little insight into how to engage in battle with Satan, a personal enemy. Thankfully, today there are an increasing number of solid, biblical books and seminary courses addressing the topic of spiritual warfare. But, unfortunately, many Christians still dismiss the importance of understanding our authority and victory over the evil one.

Another reason we are seeing the battle more clearly is that we are living in the last days. First Timothy 4:1 declares, "The Spirit clearly says that in later times some will abandon the faith and follow deceiving spirits and things taught by demons." Such verses in the Word are to be taken soberly. The aggressive, overt activities of Satan and demons are to be much more pronounced as the end times close in upon us:

> But woe to the earth and the sea, because the devil has gone down to you! He is filled with fury, because he knows that his time is short. (Revelation 12:12b)

A third reason for increased awareness of the battle is that sin abounds in our day. The more wicked humans become, the more openly and obviously the power of Satan will be displayed. This is particularly true of sins that involve occultism and sexual promiscuity. A society that is deeply characterized by pornography and other sexual sins, drugs, alcoholism, sorcery, witchcraft, and open Satan worship is a society that will see much open and obvious activity of demons.

What are believers to do in preparing themselves to meet the challenge? This book encourages believers to use warfare prayer—which I define as focusing biblical truths through prayer against the schemes and deceptions of the enemy—and other practical means to reach sure victory in the following ways.

First, believers must personally avoid and diligently guard their families from any involvement in occult practices. Ouija boards, séances, levitation, transcendental meditation, tarot cards, horoscopes, and the like should be totally avoided. Indulging curiosity about such things is like walking unarmed into the enemy's territory.

When you enter the land the LORD your God is giving you, do not learn to imitate the detestable ways of the nations there. Let no one be found among you who sacrifices their son or daughter in the fire, who practices divination or sorcery, interprets omens, engages in witchcraft, or casts spells, or who is a medium or spiritist or who consults the dead. Anyone who does these things is detestable to the LORD; because of these same detestable practices the LORD your God will drive out those nations before you. You must be blameless before the LORD your God. (Deuteronomy 18:9–13)

Second, we must also take care that we do not develop an excessive curiosity about Satan's workings. Books and films that describe the practices and orgies of witches' covens and Satan worship are out of place for believers. On the pretext of becoming informed, some well-meaning people are doing a dangerous disservice to the Christian community. Knowing the details of the rites and rituals of witchcraft is harmful and totally unnecessary. Most of us would readily see harm in a Christian's reading pornography or viewing pornographic films to better understand that area of sin, but we may fail to see harm in curiosity about witchcraft and Satanism.

Third, we must also guard against being fearfully preoccupied with Satan and his activities, thus giving him undue prominence.

Hope and courage are vital words in spiritual warfare. Courage is not only necessary in facing our relentless foe, but it is also the believer's purchased possession. Satan would like nothing better than to fill believers with dread of him and his kingdom. If he can keep his work shrouded in an aura of mystery, or if he can cloak his programs with sensationalized hocus-pocus in the minds of believers, Satan will have accomplished one of his chief aims.

"Be alert and of sober mind. Your enemy the devil prowls around like a roaring lion looking for someone to devour. Resist him, standing firm in the faith" (1 Peter 5:8–9a). Satan roars to make us afraid and thus more vulnerable, but our purchased right is courage to resist him.

Fear is one of the most prevalent reasons believers may not get involved in spiritual warfare. They hope that by ignoring the subject they will avoid having to face their enemy directly. Some say to me, "How involved do I need to become in spiritual warfare when I'm not aware of any particular problem?" My response is always to remind them that they already *are* involved if they are believers. Whether we want to be involved or not, Satan presses the battle to us in close, relentless encounter. Ephesians 6:12 declares that ours is a wrestling battle, a close, hand-to-hand struggle with Satan's highly organized kingdom.

To those who understand the formidable power of Satan's kingdom, this personal struggle is a fearsome prospect. Yet the underlying thesis of Ephesians 6 is that every believer has the certainty of victory: "and after you have done everything, to stand" (Ephesians 6:13). Prayer is the means by which we aggressively claim our strength in the Lord, appropriating the power of the Holy Spirit and putting on the whole armor of God. There is no substitute for a prayer life that brings the truth of God's Word into aggressive application. That is what Peter touched on when he told us to resist the devil, "standing firm in the faith." "The faith" is the whole body of God's truth—the absolute, eternal verities of doctrine that cannot be broken.

How courageous should believers become in applying their victory against Satan? Some evangelical Christians have resorted to exorcism of wicked spirits, even from the lives of other believers. Some cases have brought encouraging results, but at other times the benefit of that practice has been questionable indeed.

> Prayer is the means by which we aggressively claim our strength in the Lord, appropriating the power of the Holy Spirit and putting on the whole armor of God.

A story from the *Chicago Tribune* of March 27, 1975, carried this disturbing headline: "British Wife-Killer Stirs Exorcism Debate." The article reported that three hours after a man went through a seven hour "ancient ritual of exorcism," he killed and mutilated his wife. A canon of the Church of England commented on the tragic event, saying, "The . . . meddlers will dabble about in demonism not knowing what they are doing or what might happen. The damage it can do is immeasurable."[4]

Similar news accounts of the practice of exorcism of demons are common and equally controversial. What ought to be the attitude of believers toward the practice of boldly confronting demonic powers? The Lord Jesus and His disciples did on many occasions confront wicked spirits and boldly demand that they reveal their presence (Mark 5:9; Acts 16). As believers united with the Lord Jesus Christ in all of His person, position, and victory, we have authority over all wicked powers (Ephesians 1:21; 2:6; 6:10–18). There may be occasions on which a bold confronting of the enemy is necessary. The hour in which we live may force this work upon us. I sought to touch on some of those occasions and procedures in chapter 9 of *The Adversary*.

But I believe far greater emphasis should be upon the troubled believer's consistent warfare praying—the use of sound doctrine in his or her daily walk—and the practice of godly living. Individual believers must know how to exercise their authority over Satan and demons in a commanding way.

Believers must see anew their privilege and responsibility of walking victoriously as men and women of God. No believer who willfully walks in the sins of the flesh and the world can hope to escape Satan's hurt and bondage (Galatians 5:13–26; 1 John 2:15–17). Can you imagine what would happen to a soldier who took a casual stroll into his enemy's territory during the heat of war? If not killed, he would soon be surrounded and taken captive. Sadly, many believers think they can carelessly engage in sin without being vulnerable to Satan's attack. Ephesians 4:27 warns: "and do not give the devil a foothold." That's what he is looking for—a foothold to get in the door of the believer's life. He seeks to hurt, bind, and destroy us through our sin. Unless we know our way to victory, we become vulnerable.

> **Believers must see anew their privilege and responsibility of walking victoriously as men and women of God.**

Walking in Victory Over Our Flesh

Victory over fleshly sin comes first by honestly admitting our old nature's capacity to be sinful. That's why lists like Galatians 5:19–21 are given to us. God isn't surprised by our old nature. He knows its wickedness, and He wants us to know it too.

The second step in overcoming fleshly sin is to count ourselves dead to the old nature (Romans 6:5–6; Galatians 5:24). With Christ the "old man" is put to death.

The third step is to walk in the Spirit and ask Him to produce within us the fruit of His fullness (Galatians 5:22–23). He will do so as we yield to the truth of His inspired Word. Moment-by-moment application of our victory works wonders in defeating sins of the flesh.

Victory over the flesh, the world, and the devil is all provided for us. Appropriating that victory and walking in it is our responsibility. Willfully doing otherwise will lead to disaster and may require a fierce battle with Satan before freedom returns.

I believe that one of the greatest needs for the church is that believers be aware of the seriousness of our battle against Satan and the practical, spiritual help that brings us victory. Such victory must be part of our daily spiritual walk. This book will help believers in victorious warfare living and prayer.

NOTES

1. *Christianity Today,* 23, no. 6 (1979), 52.
2. Charles Cook, ed., *Daily Meditations for Prayer* (Westchester, Ill.: Good News, n.d.), 330.
3. Names of individuals used as examples in this book have been changed to protect their privacy.
4. *The Chicago Tribune,* March 27, 1975. "British wife-killer stirs exorcism debate."

PART I

THE SUPREMACY OF CHRIST

Finally, be strong in the Lord
and in his mighty power.

EPHESIANS 6:10

SATAN IS NOT INVINCIBLE

For eight wonderful months we were privileged to have in our home a lovely young lady, twenty-two years of age, who had been a heroin addict for at least five years. Before coming to us, Sandy had been detoxified in a prison hospital. She thrived in the secured environment of our Christian home. She was like a flower beginning to unfold. In her freedom from drugs, she started to see a whole new world around her, and she realized what she had missed during her bondage. She enjoyed going to church. She even made a profession of faith to receive Jesus Christ as her Savior. Her job as a nurse's aide in a local convalescent hospital became a delight as she comforted and helped the elderly patients. Her gift as a talented pianist began to return. Everything looked bright and encouraging.

All went well until one of her old friends found out where she was. He invited her to attend his sister's wedding with him. Reluctantly, at her insistence, we let her go. She later told us that on that very night she had started back on the road to drugs. Although we loved her very much, it wasn't long until we had to tell her that she would either have to live under the disciplines of our family, or she would have to leave.

The night she chose to leave we talked about her profession of faith. With unusual insight she pointed to her head and said, "I have it up here, Pastor B., but I never meant it down here," pointing to her heart. What a dark night it was for us as we watched her drive away in the new car her father was helping her purchase. Satan seemed so powerful in that moment, and we seemed so weak. A few months later I conducted her funeral. She had died of an overdose. Whether it was self-administered or forced, no one knows. Satan is indeed very powerful.

CHRIST'S POWERFUL LOVE

However, there is a brighter side to this story. During the months after Sandy left, our family never ceased to pray for her. We had frequent calls and contact with her, sometimes to help her out of a tight spot. Always she told us she loved us.

One August day, the phone rang in my office. It was our oldest daughter, Rhonda, who was visiting from out of state. She told me that Sandy was at the parsonage, wanting to see me. I dropped everything and hurried home.

I wasn't prepared for what I saw. Sandy had just walked away without release from a local hospital where she was being treated for an overdose. Her beautiful long black hair had been hacked off just below her ears by an angry boyfriend. Her face was an emaciated facsimile of the once beautiful girl who had been in our home. She was suffering not only from the overdose but from a liver ailment. Her clothing was dirty and torn. I took her in my arms and began to cry. My demonstration of love seemed to break her heart, and she sobbed and sobbed out her hurt on my shoulder.

When we were able to talk, I said to her, "Sandy, you know you are soon going to die, living this way, don't you?" She looked at me a moment, and again her eyes filled with tears as she nodded. We talked about her admission that her previous profession of faith had only been a head assent and not a heart belief. We looked at numerous Bible passages showing that eternal hope comes only to those who come heart-first to the Lord. She must of her own will acknowledge her sin and repent. She must really want to be free from the power of sin and drugs and believe that the Lord Jesus Christ could save her from all of her sins.

A terrible battle was being waged. Satan's hold upon her was being threatened, and he was fighting fiercely. At times she would seem to harden and even laugh. At other times she seemed almost to blank out. During those moments I would stop and pray aloud for her. "In the name of the Lord Jesus Christ, I bind away Satan's interference with Sandy's coming to know the Lord Jesus Christ. I invite the Holy Spirit to convict Sandy of her need of being saved from her sins. Lord Jesus Christ, open her eyes to see how much You love her."

I kept assuring Sandy that no one could make that decision for her. She had to invite Christ personally to enter her life and heart and save her soul. I had determined not to make it easy for her. I did not offer to help her pray the sinner's prayer as I had done at the time of her previous profession. I told her it had to come from her heart. She needed to pour out her heart in repentance toward God and invite the Lord Jesus to enter her life and cleanse all of her sins away.

The struggle went on for some time. One moment she seemed near deciding for Christ, the next moment she wanted to put it off until another time. Finally, I prayed a doctrinal prayer over her, claiming Christ's finished work against Satan and pleading our Lord's gracious love for Sandy.

The moment of victory came. Without any further prompting on my part, Sandy was on her knees praying. Out of her deepest soul poured forth words of sorrow for her sins and love for Christ like I have seldom heard. She expressed her longing for the Lord Jesus Christ to enter her life and free her from her sins. The tears were flowing freely, not only from her eyes but from mine as well. When she had finished her prayer, I began to pray again that the Lord would free her from all of Satan's bondage and from any demonic powers that had laid claim to her life.

Sandy was kneeling in the middle of our living room floor with her face buried in her hands on the carpet. As I prayed for her release, she began to cough profusely and to retch as though vomiting out some invisible poison. The powers of darkness that had laid such deep claim to her life for so long were leaving. It was as if wave after wave had to leave, and each time the coughing and retching would painfully convulse her body. Sandy didn't seem to really understand what was happening, but she knew it was good. I kept praying for the Lord to clean all powers of darkness out of her life and to free Sandy completely.

When Sandy finally sat up, a radiant smile lighted her whole countenance. She looked beautiful and peaceful. The shine of heaven was radiating through all the scars of sin.

"I can't believe it," she said. "I've never felt so clean inside. I'm really saved. Jesus Christ really does love me. I can't believe it. It really has happened to me." Yes, Satan is powerful, but he is not all powerful. His terrible hold on a human life had been broken again.

As I look back upon that day, I feel I made a serious misjudgment at that point. Sandy wanted to go to her parents and tell them what had happened, and we let her go. She told her parents of her decision and said, "Mom and Dad, you need never worry about me again. Even if I die tonight, I know I'm going to be in heaven."

What happened after that we do not fully know. She told her father that she was going to turn in some "very bad" people to the authorities. He was convinced that those "very bad" people could not cope with that new girl and gave her a forced drug overdose. No one really knows, but our one joy is that we have no doubt that Sandy is absent from her body and "at home with the Lord." Satan is powerful, but he is not invincible. Warfare prayer had brought one of life's most desperate wreckages through for Christ. The funeral service was a time of expressed victory. I shared the testimony of her conversion with the large gathering of her family and friends. Many of them did not know Christ and were deeply moved by the service.

UNDERESTIMATING THE ENEMY

Every time Satan appears in Scripture, there is an aura of unusual power surrounding this fallen created being. The Bible seems to indicate that God has never created any other being as powerful as Satan. Even Michael the archangel, one of the holy angels of God, was apparently no match for Satan in one direct encounter (see Jude 9). Michael had to appeal to the Lord to rebuke Satan. Satan's awesome power is further seen in the gospel accounts of the temptation of Jesus. No one can read of that encounter in the wilderness without developing a sober respect for the power and position of this archenemy of God and His kingdom. Yet, there is urgent necessity to know that Satan is not invincible. He is always "second best." He is a mere creature, no match for the Creator!

At times the battle may grow fierce, and we may feel that Satan is winning. Daniel must have felt that way when he was praying for twenty-one days for an answer to an urgent prayer of his heart (Daniel 10). He tells us that during that time he was in a state of mourning. As an expression of his deep faith toward God, Daniel implemented a limited fast and other practices of self-denial.

Daniel's prayer had reached heaven the very first day, but the answer was delayed by a powerful prince of the kingdom of Persia, who had stood in the way of the holy angel's coming with God's answer to Daniel. Only as Daniel continued to pray and fast after those twenty-one days was the holy angel able to

> Satan is not invincible. He is always "second best." He is a mere creature, no match for the Creator!

come (see Daniel 10:1–15). What if Daniel had thought Satan too powerful for him to gain an answer to this request? Perhaps the angelic messenger would not have come.

Do we give up too soon and miss the answers to our prayers? Christ may someday reveal the answer to that question, but the challenge of it ought to move us to pray with more faithful tenacity. Satan is not invincible, but we can be and ought to be. It is the Lord's will that we be provided all we need to do the Lord's will.

SATAN'S TACTICS

How deceitful Satan is when he tries to convince us that he is too powerful for us. One young professional man called me about his battle with Satan's kingdom. He was an athlete and very strong, both physically and intellectually. Yet, he had been plagued by ceaseless harassment from demonic powers. They afflicted him with annoying physical sensations and at times controlled his tongue so that he hissed like a snake. When those things happened he seemed unable to help himself.

I pointed out to him the principles of warfare as best I could over the telephone and sent him other material. For a time those things seemed to help, but then his affliction seemed to grow worse. He called me again. As he related his battle to me over the phone, he conveyed a message of despair and hopelessness. I could understand that in light of his long battle, but I knew he had to be shocked out of his despair.

After letting him talk about his battle and defeats for some time, I said, "I guess Satan really is stronger than God after all. He has you, and you might as well give up because there is no hope."

The response was instantaneous and gratifying. He saw what

I was trying to say. "That's what I'm really saying, isn't it?" he replied. "I've fallen into the trap of convincing myself that I'm defeated. Pastor, pray for me." We joined in prayer over the phone. While I was praying, the enemy tried to step up his attack, but we continued to pray and rejoice in our invincible position of victory in Christ. Their power was broken. He was able to praise the Lord for the battle and even for the defeats he suffered, rejoicing in the Lord's purpose for the prolonged battle.

A woman called and related her difficult struggle in spiritual warfare. As I tried to share with her the principles of aggressive spiritual warfare that I will outline throughout this book, she responded by assuring me that she'd done all of that for many years. She insisted that her situation was unique and difficult beyond what anyone else had experienced. She would need some very special attention before she could ever hope to be free, because Satan had such a stronghold upon her life. The secret of the enemy's strength in her life was this: She was assigning to him an invincible role in her life that he was only too happy to assume.

Once we do that we are locked into a cycle of defeat. We can't win because we know we can't. Such a person looks for someone to help her who isn't subject to Satan's "invincible" strength like she is, but even her Christian friends are helpless until the lie the person believes is renounced. Satan is not invincible. He is a defeated foe because of what our Savior did for us on the cross. The death and resurrection of our Lord Jesus Christ has ultimately defeated the enemy. Any apparent victory Satan has in our lives is only temporary. "We are more than conquerors through him [Christ] who loved us" (Romans 8:37).

Satan wants us to worship him. He took the Lord Jesus to a high mountain and showed Him "all the kingdoms of the world and their splendor. 'All this I will give you,' he said, 'if you will bow down and worship me'" (Matthew 4:8–9). If he would dare to try to get the sinless Son of God to worship him, he will employ his most subtle tricks to try to get those who belong to Christ to do the same.

Oh, very seldom will he be so brash as to try to get you to actually kneel and worship, at least not at first. He is much more subtle. He will just try to get you to exalt his power in your own thinking to the point where you regard yourself as his helpless toy. At that point, so far as you are concerned, he is indeed an invincible foe. When you fall into that trap, you are ascribing to Satan an honor that is a kind of worship, a worship composed of fear and subjection.

When I was a young man, my father would sometimes have three or more purebred bulls as part of his herd. It was inevitable that one of those bulls would have to prove in battle with the others that he was "in charge." Once that had been proved, the defeated ones would always give him the right to rule and would not challenge his authority again. That illustrates what Satan tries to do with us. When he defeats us once or several times, he is simply seeking to establish his right to rule. He wants believers to accept the fact that he is stronger than they are and that he is "in charge." Once we accept that fallacy, he has us caught in a psychological defeat that does not belong in the Christian life.

MISLED BY EXPERIENCE

There are times when experience seems to defy truth. A lady from Canada claimed to have used faithfully the principles of warfare set forth in *The Adversary*. "I've done it all," she said, "but it just doesn't work for me. I've prayed doctrinal prayers, I've read and memorized the Word, I've aggressively and consistently resisted the devil and his demons, but I'm still harassed constantly." She was discouraged, defeated, and desperately looking for some quick relief. She lamented that there didn't seem to be anyone near who was interested in helping her. Her experience of battle was a direct challenge to the truth of God. She was so defeated that she was not even attending church.

As we talked, I asked her if she had ever thanked her Lord for the battle. I asked her if she had ever prayed that the Lord would teach her everything He wanted her to learn through this prolonged battle. She confessed that she had not. Her attitude had been that this battle with Satan's kingdom was all bad and that the only thing God would want for her would be immediate and total victory. Yet when she saw that God might want to teach her stability and faithfulness in spite of the battle and in the very midst of the greatest defeat she had ever experienced—for He can bring good out of any situation—it opened up an entire new vista for her.

We talked about her neglect of church attendance and fellowship with the body of believers as an admission to Satan's victory. Her "giving up" on warfare praying and saying that warfare principles were "not working" were admissions that Satan was winning. She needed to stand upon the truth and not let the experience of her battle remove her from it.

That is what the apostle Paul keeps emphasizing in his great doctrinal exhortations of Romans 5 and 6. We must stand upon truth and not allow subjective experience to challenge the absolute truth. Only as we do that will the subjective experience begin to harmonize with truth. Subjective experience is never to be trusted as a valid establisher of spiritual truth. The revealed Word of God establishes truth.

In Romans 6:5–10 the apostle Paul expounds the truth that each believer is united with Christ in His total victory over sin and death and Satan. That is an infallible truth upon which each believer is responsible to stand. This is an unchanging, eternal truth that we are responsible to appropriate and live out in our everyday lives. Satan will ceaselessly seek to challenge the truth. He will bring all the harassment he can muster into your experience to make you think that for you this just doesn't work. He keeps saying by your experience that sin is too strong and he can and will reign in your life.

What is Paul's answer to such attack? "In the same way, count yourselves dead to sin but alive to God in Christ Jesus. Therefore do not let sin reign in your mortal body so that you obey its evil desires" (Romans 6:11–12).

Paul's challenge is repeatedly communicated in similar doctrinal passages. We must stand upon truth. Our responsibility is to affirm as fact that we are "dead" to the rule and reign of sin, of death, and of Satan in our lives.

We are "alive to God." Our Lord is ruling. Our responsibility is to "not let sin reign." Sin and Satan can reign only if we "let" them do so. We "let" them reign when we accept the idea that "it doesn't work" or we neglect "assembling together" because the experience of battle is too great. The moment we allow Satan an invincible role in our lives because of our experience of battle and our experience of defeat, we are letting him reign. Victory comes because we have certainty of our victory through our Lord Jesus Christ.

There is no point at which the believer needs to "cave in" and admit defeat at the hands of Satan's craft and power. There is hope and victory available for the most defeated. The church at Laodicea illustrates this point. That body of believers had succumbed to Satan's deception. Spiritual lukewarmness had taken over. That church felt very self-sufficient and spiritually victorious in its own strength. They were saying: "I am rich; I have acquired wealth and do not need a thing." They were so blinded by Satan's clever deception that they didn't know they were "wretched, pitiful, poor, blind and naked" (Revelation 3:17). Yet, even to people so totally deceived, the Lord Jesus offered full access to His victory.

I counsel you to buy from me gold refined by fire, so that you may be rich, and white garments so that you may clothe yourself and the shame of your nakedness may not be seen, and

salve to anoint your eyes, so that you may see.
Those whom I love, I reprove and discipline, so be zealous
and repent. Behold, I stand at the door and knock. If anyone
hears my voice and opens the door, I will come in to him and
eat with him, and he with me. (Revelation 3:18–20 ESV)

That great offer and assurance belongs to every believer. No matter how far Satan has come in deceiving and controlling us, we can have gold tried in the fires of refining; white, clean garments; and salve of healing to remove our spiritual blindness. Close, intimate, in-the-heart fellowship with Christ is there to be claimed. Satan is not invincible, but Christ is, and the believer is invincible in Him.

A PRAYER OF VICTORY

Loving Heavenly Father, I praise You that Satan is a defeated foe. I rejoice that his defeat was accomplished by the Lord Jesus Christ in His sinless life, His death, burial, resurrection, and ascension into glory. I look forward to that day when the Lord Jesus Christ's rule has come in its fullness, when Satan is bound in the bottomless pit. I know that Satan will ultimately be forever consigned to the lake of fire prepared for him and his angels. I rejoice that You have given to me, in my union with the Lord Jesus Christ, complete victory over Satan today.

I enter into my victory aggressively and claim my place as more than a conqueror through Him that loved me. I refuse to admit continuing defeat by Satan in any area of my life. He cannot and will not rule over me. In Christ, I am dead to the enemy's rule. I affirm that the grace and mercy of God rule in all areas of my life through my union with the Lord Jesus Christ. Grant to me the grace to affirm Your victory even when experiences of life seem to say otherwise.

I thank You for these battles and all that You are seeking to accomplish in Your wisdom and design for my life. I accept the battle and rejoice in Your purpose. I willingly accept and desire to profit from all of Your purpose in letting Satan's kingdom get at me. I reject all of Satan's purpose. Through the victory of my Lord and Savior I stand resolute and strong upon the certainty of my victory. In confidence I look to You, Lord Jesus Christ. When Your purpose for this trial is fulfilled, I know that it shall fade into the dimness of forgotten battles and a defeated enemy. Through the precious name of the Lord Jesus Christ, it shall be so. Amen.

2

KEEPING A
SOVEREIGN
PERSPECTIVE

A bove everything else, Christians need to cultivate a faith that
establishes them as winners. This is all-important. Anything
less gives Satan and his kingdom a devastating advantage.

Coach Bear Bryant in his lifetime became a football legend.
More than anything, he is remembered as a winner. At the end
of his thirty-eight-season career he held six national champion-
ships and more victories than any other coach in college football
history at that time.

Victor Gold, in a tribute to Bryant's career, wrote of him in
the February 19, 1983, issue of *National Review*: "Like all authentic Southern legends, he was of the soil. 'If I hadn't found football,'
he once said, 'I'd have ended up behind a mule, just like my daddy.
But I'll tell you one thing. I'd have plowed the straightest furrow
in Arkansas.'"[1]

Somebody once asked him, "Don't you consider yourself an
innovator? A stylesetter?"

"No," he said, "I ain't nothin' but a winner." The winning career
and philosophy of life espoused by Bear Bryant says something
important to believers. We need to know that through grace and
redemption's victory we are nothing but winners.

Habakkuk lived in a day much like our own. He saw moral and spiritual degeneracy, expressed in violence and injustice, everywhere he looked. In his prayers he cried:

How long, LORD, must I call for help, but you do not listen? Or cry out to you, "Violence!" but you do not save? Why do you make me look at injustice? Why do you tolerate wrongdoing? Destruction and violence are before me; there is strife, and conflict abounds. (Habakkuk 1:2–3)

A prophet in our day might have the same lament when viewing the contemporary world scene. Satan's program includes a cacophony of violence, injustice, and brutality. Promising much, Satan always delivers little. The more he exerts his sway, the more frightening and chaotic matters become in individual lives and in society as well. Satan is a usurper. He tries to hold power by force without any right to do so. That is why it is important to know our biblical and legal ground of authority when under attack by Satan's kingdom.

YOUR LEGAL RIGHTS

Dear friends of ours went through some incredibly dark days. The wife would occasionally suffer seizures, much like those of an epileptic, particularly at night, with no apparent medical explanation. Doctors believed the seizures were generated by some sort of anxiety attack, but they had never seen it manifested in that way. Psychologists explained that the attacks were from repressed anger. Our friends revealed the problem to me as we discussed spiritual insights into their trying time.

We had reason to suspect demonic causes for the seizures, but it is best to be cautious in such delicate emotional situations. Hasty and simplified answers can be not only unfair but also very harmful. Yet by observation and experience, I had come to know that such attacks *could* certainly be demonic in origin. Satan cleverly intensifies human weakness. He desires to push to the ultimate any problem that originates in human weakness. Psychological problems we might otherwise work through rather easily can almost destroy us when intensified by Satan.

We discussed the possibility of Satan's involvement. Not only were the seizures painful, but they were frightening as well. We carefully considered the believer's biblical authority to refuse Satan the right to rule any area of our lives. In Romans 6 the family saw their privilege and responsibility to "not let sin reign in your mortal body so that you obey its evil desires" (Romans 6:12).

A careful procedure was planned. The next time a seizure began, they were immediately to challenge any of Satan's involvement by forbidding him to rule in this way. We talked of how the husband could come to his wife's rescue by challenging any spirit of darkness behind the seizure. He was to say, "In the name of the Lord Jesus Christ and by the power of His blood, I resist any spirit of darkness that is trying to cause my wife to have a seizure. I forbid you to do it. I command you to leave our presence and to go where the Lord Jesus Christ sends you." He was urged to insist repeatedly until the seizure was broken. His wife was encouraged as best she was able to repeat the challenge her husband addressed against Satan.

As our friends utilized this strategy, the seizures ceased completely. In this case demons had indeed been involved and were seeking to intensify a human weakness.

Our subtle enemy will do anything to try to deceive us into his control. If he can convince us that our problems are not of his doing, he can continue his work. While blaming the devil for all our troubles is never wise, neither is dismissing his involvement too quickly.

Imagine one day you answer the door and there stands a

powerfully built man who boldly pushes his way into your house before you can object. His towering size and forceful voice overwhelm you. He makes himself right at home and takes over. You try to find out why he is there, but he is evasive, saying he is your friend and just wants to be neighborly.

The man of the house tires of the intrusion and suggests that the family would appreciate his leaving so that they can have dinner. "Oh," says the big man, "that's a great idea. When do we eat?"

Baffled by this brash intrusion but respecting the strong man's size, the head of the house hesitates to throw the intruder out. Dinner is served, and the big fellow eats most of it. After dinner he proceeds into the living room and monopolizes the conversation. The family grows increasingly uncomfortable, but the man's size, piercing eyes, and powerful voice intimidate everyone.

Dad finally suggests that it is getting late and that perhaps the man should leave because it is time to go to bed. The big man laughs and says that he is tired too; he has decided to stay and sleep in the main bedroom. By this time everyone is exasperated, but what can be done? One sweep of his powerful hand would wipe them all out. He goes into the bedroom and takes over. He is too big for any of them to throw out. Intimidated, they are forced to let him stay.

How unthinkable that any of us would let that happen. Big or not, the man has to go. He's an intruder, a usurper. He has no right to enter, let alone stay. What can we do to get rid of him?

If we are wise, we will call the police and force him to leave. He may be too big for us to handle, but all the authority of the law and government are on our side. If it takes a whole militia to do the job, justice and authority will not allow him to stay. Yet we must initiate the action. Our requests don't get him to leave. Threats only make him laugh because of his strength and size.

We are impotent against his strength. He would stay forever if we fail to appeal to legal authority.

Satan is that kind of foe. That is how he operates against Christians, though he is much more subtle. Ephesians 4:27 warns us not to give the devil a foothold. He pushes his way into our lives, where he has no legal right to be. He will try to convince us that our weakness, demonstrated by our sins and failures, gives him that right. Once we have opened the door by giving in to a particular sin, he insists that he will stay around as long as he desires. Intimidated by his power and guilt-ridden by our sins, we fearfully conclude that maybe he does have the right after all.

We are not talking about a Christian's being possessed by Satan. The apostle Paul was certainly not possessed by Satan, but he was able to experience deep affliction and some sort of demonic oppression that greatly troubled him.

Even if I should choose to boast, I would not be a fool, because I would be speaking the truth. But I refrain, so no one will think more of me than is warranted by what I do or say, or because of these surpassingly great revelations. Therefore, in order to keep me from becoming conceited, I was given a thorn in my flesh, a messenger of Satan, to torment me. Three times I pleaded with the Lord to take it away from me. But he said to me, "My grace is sufficient for you, for my power is made perfect in weakness." Therefore I will boast all the more gladly about my weaknesses, so that Christ's power may rest on me.
(2 Corinthians 12:6–9)

There are two important lessons to be drawn from Paul's experience. Of first importance is always to pray to God when we sense Satan's intrusions into our lives.

Paul knew that Satan had no *legal* right to be a distracting influence in his life. He had every right to "resist the devil" with the certainty that Satan would have to "flee from him." He had all authority, every legal right, to insist that this demonically caused affliction leave him. All the authority of Christ, in the Savior's Person and finished work, belonged to Paul as a result of his union with Christ. Satan had no legal claim on Paul. Neither does he have any legal claim on other believers. That is the very heart of the message of the finished work of Christ. Hebrews 2:14–15 sums it up for us: "Since the children have flesh and blood, he too shared in their humanity so that by his death he might break the power of him who holds the power of death—that is, the devil— and free those who all their lives were held in slavery by their fear of death." The Lord Jesus Christ's work frees us legally and completely from Satan's claims.

There is yet another important lesson to learn from Paul's experience. We must allow our Lord to be sovereign. For Paul to insist upon his personal "legal" rights in his case would have been an insult to his Lord. In His sovereignty, the Lord had a purpose in allowing Satan to afflict the apostle. This illustrates a vital principle of spiritual warfare. In our spiritual battles, we must always keep our Lord first in importance. Even in direct battle with Satan, our primary dealings are with God. He has a purpose in our struggle with the forces of darkness that is for our good and His glory.

That fact is never more clear than in the Old Testament account of Job. All of Job's troubles, pain, and torment were satanically caused. Yet, Job kept all of his attention centered upon his Lord as he worked through his horrendous trials.

Job knew a very important principle about a righteous man's dealings with the devil. He knew that his Lord had a sovereign purpose in the struggle. It was the same awareness that Paul accepted and delighted in.

When we are battling with Satan and the powers of darkness, two important dimensions need to be kept in view: First, we must know that because we are united with Christ, we have full authority to resist Satan and to force him to leave our presence. Yet at the same moment we must be willing to accept our Lord's sovereign purpose for allowing us to experience the battle, even if it is prolonged.

> Even in direct battle with Satan, our primary dealings are with God. He has a purpose in our struggle with the forces of darkness that is for our good and His glory.

I often urge those facing an intense struggle with Satan to say two things. The first expresses positive faith toward the Lord: "In the name of the Lord Jesus Christ, I accept every purpose my Lord has for allowing me to experience this fierce battle with Satan. I desire to profit and to learn all of my Lord's purpose in this battle." The second rejects Satan's purpose: "In the name of the Lord Jesus Christ and by the power of His blood, I reject every purpose of Satan and his kingdom in afflicting me in this battle. I command every wicked spirit behind this affliction to leave my presence and to go where the Lord Jesus Christ sends him."

Sometimes when we are under affliction from the enemy, our only thought is to have the experience end. Countless times people have called me wanting to learn a quick formula for instant deliverance. It is painfully difficult but eminently necessary for those suffering such affliction to remember to keep the Lord's sovereignty in view. Sometimes the Lord plans to set people free immediately, but at other times He, in His sovereignty, may choose for the battle to be prolonged. Yielding to our Lord is always paramount. It is His will that needs to be done and not our own, and we often grow the most in life's most painful experiences.

Though I have lost the source, I recall reading a story that was related by Festo Kivengere, the renowned Anglican Bishop of Uganda. During the Ugandan rule of the dictator Idi Amin, many Ugandans were killed for the slightest offense—real or imagined—against the government. Many of those killed were Ugandan Christians.

As one believer was being fastened to a tree to be executed by a firing squad, he asked to be allowed to speak to his tormentors. Looking directly into their eyes, he declared with a strong voice, "I love you, and I love my country! As I die, I would like to sing to you." He smiled, and the words of his song flowed out with calm assurance: "Out of my bondage, sorrow and night, Jesus, I come; Jesus I come." While he was singing that hymn, the shots rang out and he died, but he died an invincible Christian. He was "more than a conqueror." He was nothing but a winner.

While pastoring in southern California, I received a heart-breaking report of a tragic accident involving some dear friends of ours. Tim and I had served together as pastors for neighboring churches in another state for nearly twelve years. We had grown very close, serving in the same denomination. As prayer partners, we shared each other's joys and burdens. It was a shock to learn of the accident. A drunk driver had veered across the dividing line and crashed head on into the small car Tim was driving. His wife was instantly killed, and Tim was in critical condition.

I could feel Tim's sorrow and pain. As I made my way to the intensive care unit of the hospital, I wondered what I would say. What could I communicate that would minister to one grieving and crushed by such sorrow and physical hurt? Tim and his wife had been so close. Theirs was a bright example of Christian marriage at its best.

Walking toward Tim's bed, I noted the extensive life-support equipment. The attending nurse related the seriousness of Tim's condition and asked me to make my visit brief. Tears filled my eyes as Tim's eyes met mine. Trying to control my emotions, I took his one uninjured hand in mine and just held it a moment. "Tim," I finally was able to say, "I'm so sorry. I love you very much." Though he couldn't speak with his voice, his eyes and countenance spoke eloquently. That sparkle of faith and smile of confidence I had known so well still greeted me. Something radiated from within him. It was like a shining fire. I had come to comfort Tim with a few Scripture promises, a word of love, and a prayer of support. Yet in that moment the ministry of the Holy Spirit flowed from him to me. He was moving through that tragedy as "more than a conqueror." He was experiencing what it is to be invincible. I left knowing that he would recover and that his life would continue to manifest God's strength. He too was nothing but a winner.

The apostle Paul ends his epistle to the Ephesians by setting forth four keys to strength that enable believers to always remain winners. No matter how fierce the battle becomes, no matter how much pressure Satan brings to bear, no matter that to human perspective it seems otherwise, we will remain triumphant as we utilize what God has provided.

FOUR KEYS TO VICTORY OVER SATAN

The four keys to victory over Satan are:

1. the believer's union with Christ,
2. the Person of the Holy Spirit,
3. the whole armor of God, and
4. the allness of prayer.

We shall look at each of these more in detail in subsequent chapters, but it seems vital to establish a general understanding of each early in our thinking.

The Believer's Union with Christ

"Finally, be strong in the Lord" (Ephesians 6:10a). Our strength and assurance of victory center on our being "in the

Lord." Our inseparable bond to all of His person and work assures us of being nothing but winners.

The Person of the Holy Spirit

"Finally, be strong . . . in his mighty power" (Ephesians 6:10). Just as the first phrase speaks of the entire Person and work of the Lord Jesus Christ, so the second phrase speaks of the Person and work of the Holy Spirit. Jesus' final words to His disciples focused on the origin of power in the life of a believer: "But you will receive power when the Holy Spirit comes on you" (Acts 1:8). It is through the Holy Spirit that we experience "the power of His might." We shall need to understand how to appropriate the Person and work of the Holy Spirit in our warfare.

The Whole Armor of God

The third key is the supplying of the whole armor of God for both protection and projection. "Put on the full armor of God, so that you can take your stand against the devil's schemes" (Ephesians 6:11). Each element of the armor plays a unique and strategic role in securing and maintaining the believer's victory. Victorious believers will maintain a growing appreciation of the armor throughout their lifetime. We must acquaint ourselves with our armor.

The Allness of Prayer

The fourth key carries an importance all its own because it is the means by which a believer appropriates the other three. "And pray in the Spirit on all occasions with all kinds of prayers and requests. With this in mind, be alert and always keep on praying for all the Lord's people" (Ephesians 6:18).

I know of no better way to stand in the victory of our union with Christ than to pray. Applying the work of the Holy Spirit in our daily lives is as related to prayer as air is related to breathing.

The practice of prayer is absolutely essential to putting on one's armor. We will study more fully the use of prayer and its essential role in ensuring that as believers we remain winners.

A PRAYER OF SURRENDER TO HIS SOVEREIGN PLAN

Loving Heavenly Father, enable me to keep all things within the perspective of Your sovereignty. Grant to me the wisdom to know that the fierceness of the battle is not evidence of defeat. Help me to thank and praise You for Your purpose in each phase of the battle. I reject all of Satan's purpose for his attack upon me, but I accept all of Your sovereign plan and purpose. I thank You for what You are doing by allowing Satan's kingdom to war against me. Use the battle to refine, deepen, mature, humble, and increase my faith.

Grant to me the insight and understanding to know my victory. I desire that the roots of my assurance of victory would go down deeply into the essential doctrines of Your Word. I want to see myself as being invincibly strong through my union with Christ, the Person and work of the Holy Spirit, the wholeness of Your provided armor, and the allness of prayer. Teach me how to appropriate my victory in a practical, daily practice. These things I ask in the name of my Lord Jesus Christ. Amen.

NOTES

1. © 1983 by National Review, Inc., 150 East 35 St., New York, NY 10016. Reprinted with permission.

3

THE BELIEVER'S UNION WITH CHRIST

Finally, be strong in the Lord and in his mighty power.
(Ephesians 6:10)

That is an order issued by a trained captain of warfare, the apostle Paul. It is a strong word given by the Holy Spirit to Christian soldiers, who are facing a powerful enemy. What a command that is! The use of the Greek imperative makes it a command we are to obey. The theological implications are obvious. We are meant to be invincible in our warfare, and we should settle for nothing less.

In Romans 8, after revealing the lofty position of the believer—that he has been predestined, called, justified, and glorified—Paul dramatically declares the invincible strength of the believer in warfare. "What, then, shall we say in response to these things? If God is for us, who can be against us?" (Romans 8:31).

The answer he expects from us is a shout of victory. "Absolutely no one!" Not even Satan himself can successfully come against believers who know their ground of victory. A few verses later Paul restates that assurance of victory: "No, in all these things we are more than conquerors through him who loved us.

For I am convinced that neither death nor life, neither angels nor demons, neither the present nor the future, nor any powers, neither height nor depth, nor anything else in all creation, will be able to separate us from the love of God that is in Christ Jesus our Lord" (Romans 8:37–39).

No wonder this man who knew the strength that belonged to him could say, "I can do all this through him who gives me strength" (Philippians 4:13). He knew he was invincible in battle. Everything standing in the way of God's will for his life had to move aside—Satan, demons, and any other power.

Knowing we are spiritually invincible in fulfilling God's will for our lives is a necessary prerequisite to effective warfare praying. Satan is a successful liar. He spares no subtle tactic to try to intimidate believers and to convince them that they are weak. Satan wants us to think that we are defenseless in light of his awesome power. Unless we know the biblical basis of our invincible position, he will doubtlessly succeed in convincing us that we are no match for his assaults.

Several years ago, a man came to me who was experiencing a severe battle with the powers of darkness. They had been tormenting him for many years in numerous ways. He often had horrible dreams full of sadistic violence or vile sexual orgy. During his waking hours, he heard cruel voices that urged him to do hideous acts that revolted his sensitive Christian spirit. At other times, he experienced physical pain that seemed to be caused by the powers of darkness. Psychiatric care and counseling had not been able to relieve his torment.

As I counseled him, I sought to lead him to aggressively resist the assaults on the ground of his own spiritual authority as a Christian. Believers must fearlessly and aggressively resist such attacks by using this type of approach:

"In the name of the Lord Jesus Christ, I come against the power of darkness causing these voices to suggest these hideous acts to me. *[Be sure to name whatever symptom you are experiencing.]* I come against you in the power of my union with the Lord Jesus Christ, and through His precious blood I resist you. I bind your whole kingdom to you. *[Wicked spirits are structured much like a military organization with leaders and others who follow the leader's orders.]* I bind you from working, and I command you and your kingdom to leave me and to go where the Lord Jesus Christ sends you."

When I first suggested this approach to the man, his response was, "Oh, I would be afraid to do that. Satan might overwhelm me. I'm not very strong spiritually, and I don't think I would dare to ever speak against Satan like that."

That is a classic example of how easily we succumb to Satan's lies. This man had an inadequate concept of his biblical position. He didn't know his true authority. He didn't see his position as a conqueror. Yet through study of the Word and patient encouragement, he was eventually able to begin to claim his victory. When he did, the problem immediately began to cease.

It is important that our vision of being invincible rests upon the solid truth of God's Word. Our authority must have biblical foundation. Presumptuous courage that originates in some wrong belief will not only lead us to lose many battles, but it also puts us in danger. The battle we face is not small or trivial. When we talk about being invincible and able to defeat Satan's kingdom, we must not let such knowledge cause us to become careless. Our invincibility over Satan's kingdom does not mean that his power is altogether insignificant. We must always remember that Satan's power is indeed great, second only to the power of God Himself. Jude 8 and 9 warn us never to treat lightly the power of our enemy: "In the very same way, on the strength of the dreams those ungodly people pollute their own bodies, reject authority and heap abuse on celestial beings. But even the archangel Michael, when he was disputing with the devil about the body of Moses, did not himself dare to condemn or slander, but said, 'The Lord rebuke you!' "

The seven sons of Sceva, a Jewish chief priest, learned that lesson in a painful way. While Paul was at Ephesus, these usurpers tried to use Paul's formula without knowing the truth behind it. As they tried to deal with wicked spirits, they said, "In the name of the Jesus whom Paul preaches,

> I command you to come out" (Acts 19:13). The results were tragic: "One day the evil spirit answered them, 'Jesus I know, and Paul I know about, but who are you?' Then the man who had the evil spirit jumped on them and overpowered them all. He gave them such a beating that they ran out of the house naked and bleeding" (Acts 19:15–16).

COURAGE IN CHRIST

Believers need courage. They must not be fearful; yet, they must be sure that their courage is resting upon that which really makes them invincible. Ephesians 6:10 says, "Finally, be strong in the Lord and in his mighty power." That little phrase *in the Lord* is one of the most important we will ever come to understand. It is the very cornerstone to our knowing that we are invincible in spiritual warfare.

> Being "in Christ" is a doctrinal fact, an absolute truth that grants to the believer a new stance.

The phrases *in the Lord, in Christ,* or their equivalent appear more than forty times in the book of Ephesians alone. Such repetition indicates that such phrases are not convenient clichés.

Every Christian is inseparably united with the Lord Jesus Christ. We are placed by God into oneness with Jesus' Person and work. Christ's work belongs to every believer by right of intimate union. God's Word states concisely and decisively: "Therefore, if anyone is in Christ, he is a new creation. The old has passed away; the new has come" (2 Corinthians 5:17 ESV). Being "in Christ" is a doctrinal fact, an absolute truth that grants to the believer a new stance. The old bondage and fear of Satan has been broken. All of Christ's victory has become ours.

WHAT IT MEANS TO BE "IN CHRIST"

What does it mean to be "in Christ"? What is there about this relationship that makes us invincibly strong? How can we use this truth in warfare prayer? How can it make our resistance to Satan victorious?

Mighty in Victory

First, being "in Christ" means that we stand in the mighty victory of the *name* of the Lord Jesus Christ because of what His death and resurrection accomplished for us. What a great source of power for victory His name represents! Philippians 2:9–11 conveys to us something of the power of His name:

Therefore God exalted him to the highest place and gave him the name that is above every name, that at the name of Jesus every knee should bow, in heaven and on earth and under the earth, and every tongue acknowledge that Jesus Christ is Lord, to the glory of God the Father.

His is a name "above every name"—that speaks of a place of security and invincible strength. "Every knee should bow" in submission to the power of that name. Satan himself and all of his kingdom are included.

It is important daily to pray the security and strength of His name over your personal life, your family, and the call of God upon your life. It is in the name of the Lord Jesus Christ that we are strong and invincible.

United to Christ in His Victory

To be "in Christ" also means we are united to Christ in all of the victory that He achieved in His redemptive work. At the moment of conversion, God puts the believer into all the victory Christ achieved in *His incarnation.* One of the most astounding truths about the redemptive work of Christ is that in the Person of Christ, God Himself became a human being. The humanity of Christ remains one of the great wonders of eternity. It was in His incarnate form, as one of us, that our Lord Jesus Christ achieved our redemption and totally defeated the kingdom of darkness (Hebrews 2:14–15).

First John 4:2–3 states:

> "This is how you can recognize the Spirit of God: Every spirit that acknowledges that Jesus Christ has come in the flesh is from God, but every spirit that does not acknowledge Jesus is not from God. This is the spirit of the antichrist, which you have heard is coming and even now is already in the world."

The truth concerning God's entering the world in the Person of Christ, that God was in Christ, that God Himself became a human being is a great defeat, a devastating threat to Satan's kingdom. John tells us that is a truth so threatening and devastating to the kingdom of darkness that fallen beings will not freely admit that Jesus Christ has come in human flesh.

Victory over Satan belongs to us through our union with

Christ in His incarnation. That victory is experienced by those who appropriate and use that mighty truth against our enemy. It is powerfully defeating to our adversary when we focus the truth of our union with Christ in His incarnation against Satan and his kingdom through prayer. Our hope for the daily favor and blessing of God upon us is uniquely related to the truth that we are included in the perfect worthiness of Christ in His humanity. He always lived a human life that was worthy of God's best blessings. Though tempted in every way, He remained without sin (Hebrews 4:15). He was always in fellowship with the heavenly Father, always utterly holy and worthy of God's best. As we walk in this world, His worthy human life belongs to us. It is ours. God sees us in Him. We do not expect those manifold blessings of God day by day because of how good and successful *we* are in living a perfect life. No, we expect His blessings because our incarnate Savior lived a perfectly worthy life, and we are "in Christ."

The Victory Won by His Death

To be "in Christ" also means that we experience the effects of and victory accomplished by *His death.* The sufferings and the death of our Lord Jesus Christ are equally vital to our invincible position of victory in battle.

> "Since the children have flesh and blood, he too shared in their humanity so that by his death he might break the power of him who holds the power of death—that is, the devil—and free those who all their lives were held in slavery by their fear of death" (Hebrews 2:14–15).

In His plan of redemption, God puts believers into the death of Christ with all of its victory over our enemies. It remains for us to aggressively lay hold of our union with Christ in His death and apply it as a part of our responsibility in invincible warfare. This is conveyed to us in passages like Romans 6:11–12: "In the same way, count yourselves dead to sin but alive to God in Christ Jesus. Therefore do not let sin reign in your mortal body so that you obey its evil desires."

The fact that we are commanded not to let sin reign in our mortal bodies is evidence that even believers can have this problem. If believers do not appropriate and apply the truth of their union with Christ in His death, sin in its various expressions will rule. We are responsible to "count," to affirm as truth the fact that we are dead to sin's reign. We are united with Christ in His death. Because of that doctrinal fact, we are dead to the rule of sin but alive to God's reign.

The cross and the blood of our Savior are a great threat to Satan's kingdom. Through the cross, Jesus Christ brought Satan's kingdom to nothing. As believers aggressively apply the death of Christ, claiming all of its benefits to their personal lives, to their families, and to their ministry for the Lord, they too become invincible with Christ in His death. "And having disarmed the powers and authorities, he made a public spectacle of them, triumphing over them by the cross" (Colossians 2:15).

The Victory in His Resurrection

To be "in Christ" also means we participate in *His resurrection*. The same mighty power that raised up our Lord Jesus Christ from the grave belongs to us and is ours. No wonder that long after he had become a believer, Paul would write to the Philippians and say, "I want to know Christ—yes, to know the power of his resurrection and participation in his sufferings, becoming like him in his death, and so, somehow, attaining to the resurrection from the dead" (Philippians 3:10–11). Being "in the Lord" means that mighty power of the resurrection is ours to be known and used to make us invincible in our warfare.

Seated with Christ in the Heavenlies

Further, to be "in Christ" means we are seated with Christ in the heavenlies. "And God raised us up with Christ and seated us with him in the heavenly realms in Christ Jesus" (Ephesians 2:6).

We are also told in Ephesians that after His resurrection, the Lord Jesus Christ was seated at God's right hand:

> *I pray that the eyes of your heart may be enlightened in order that you may know the hope to which he has called you, the riches of his glorious inheritance in his holy people, and his incomparably great power for us who believe. That power is the same as the mighty strength he exerted when he raised Christ from the dead and seated him at his right hand in the heavenly realms, far above all rule and authority, power and dominion, and every name that is invoked, not only in the present age but also in the one to come. And God placed all things under his feet and appointed him to be head over everything for the church, which is his body, the fullness of him who fills everything in every way.* (Ephesians 1:18–23)

The ascension of Christ into glory was the sealing moment of His finished triumph, a demonstration of His supreme victory "far above all rule and authority." We are seated with Christ there, and our "in Christ" position is a truth demonstrating our "in the Lord" authority to resist the devil and to defeat him. We are united with Christ in all His ascended authority and power.

Applying the Truth

One final thought needs to be stressed. To be strong, invincible "in the Lord" means we know and apply the truth that we are united with Christ in His watchful *headship* over His church. He is our great High Priest and the glorified Shepherd of His sheep. How beautiful it is to know that we are united to our living Savior who is building His church, to know that He has said, "'Never will I leave you; never will I forsake you.' So we say with confidence, 'The Lord is my helper; I will not be afraid'" (Hebrews 13:5–6).

Phrases like "in Christ" and "in the Lord" help us know that it is God's will that we be invincibly strong. Satan's roaring never need frighten us if we are "in Christ."

Dear warrior, you can stand mighty in your position in Christ through:

- His mighty name
- His incarnate, redemptive work
- His death
- His resurrection
- His seat at God's right hand
- His headship over the church

A woman shared with me a fascinating story that illustrates the nature of our invincible warfare when aggressively applied.

In her youth she had attended a fine Bible college, where she gained a good foundation of biblical knowledge. In later years as she reared her family, she admitted that her faith became more of a practice of habit than a vital life of day-by-day walking with Christ. Though an active participant in a Bible preaching church, she lacked a warm, consistent relationship with her Lord. She became an "institutional" Christian. Such professional Christianity can often lead to disaster, as it did in her case.

Her relationship with her husband left her wanting more. Her three teenage children were headed for disaster. Her oldest son was hopelessly caught in the drug scene and was drifting without any goals in life. Her teenage daughter was involved in a flirtatious affair with a married man and refused to heed warning against the dangers and tragedies of her course in life. Her youngest son, still in high school, was headed the same way as his older brother. This

Christian mother was desperate and didn't know what she could do to remedy the tragedy of her and her family's life.

She called me one day to tell me that she had read *The Adversary*.

The challenge to practice doctrinal praying as set forth in that book had moved her heart. She began to focus such prayer for her home and children. Five months later she was calling to share with me the results.

Her oldest son had renounced his involvement with drugs and was making plans to attend a Bible college. Her daughter had ended the relationship with the married man and was nearing engagement with a dedicated Christian. Her youngest son had renewed his commitment to Christ and was actively participating in the leadership of his church youth group. Joyfully she shared other dramatic spiritual results that God was bringing into her life and home. Although doctrinal praying does not always produce such dramatic results, I relate this account as a testimony to the practical benefits of a vision to be invincible in warfare prayer. Focusing the victory of Christ upon our personal lives, upon our families, and upon our unique area of ministry will always reap significant rewards.

A PRAYER FOR CLAIMING OUR UNION WITH CHRIST

Loving Heavenly Father, I praise Your name. I've come to see that it is Your will that I be invincibly strong in my spiritual warfare. I praise You, Lord, that You have placed me "in Christ." By faith I express my desire to abide in the protection and blessing of the mighty name of the Lord Jesus Christ. I pray the omnipotent power of His name over my family and the ministry to which You have called me. I pray the name of the Lord Jesus Christ against

Satan and all that his kingdom would do to hinder God's plan for my life.

I focus my prayer on my union with Christ in His incarnation. I joyfully confess that Jesus Christ has come in human flesh to win my victory for me. I pray all of the triumphs that the Lord Jesus achieved in His humanity against all of Satan's subtle wiles and crafty deceits. I pray the victories of the incarnation over all areas of my life and ministry.

I praise You for the cross and death of the Lord Jesus Christ, desiring all the benefits of His death to focus upon my life, my family, and my ministry. I affirm that my death with Christ can defeat the control and rule of sin, death, and Satan. I desire the shed blood of Christ to work against all that Satan is doing to hinder me.

I hunger to learn more deeply what it means to experience the power of His resurrection. Just as I desire to be dead to the reign of sin, so I long to live according to the fact that I am alive unto God through the power of the resurrection. In the mighty power that raised up the Lord Jesus Christ from the dead, enable me to walk in the newness of life available to me.

Heavenly Father, it will always remain a marvel to me that You have seated me with Christ in the heavenly realm, far above all principalities and powers. Humbly I use the authority of my union with the ascended Christ to pull down all of Satan's plans formed against me personally, all of his plans formed against my family, and all of his plans formed against God's appointed plan for my life.

Thank You, Lord Jesus Christ, that in Your glorified position at the Father's right hand, You are leading Your church and shepherding Your sheep. I deliberately submit to Your lordship of my life and ministry. I acknowledge that everything that is good about my life, home, and ministry is because of Your lordship and gracious blessing. By faith I claim my right in Christ to be invincibly strong and victorious in Your complete salvation. I refuse to be discouraged. I reject all emotions that make me feel defeated. I choose to live as one who is more than a conqueror through Jesus Christ my Lord. In the name of my Lord Jesus Christ, I pray with thanksgiving. Amen.

PART II

THE WORK OF THE HOLY SPIRIT

But very truly I tell you, it is for your
good that I am going away.
Unless I go away, the Advocate will not come to you;
but if I go, I will send him to you.

When he comes, he will prove the world to be in the
wrong about sin and righteousness and judgment:
about sin, because people do not believe in me; about
righteousness, because I am going to the Father, where you
can see me no longer; and about judgment, because the
prince of this world now stands condemned.

JOHN 16:7–11

4

THE PERSON OF THE HOLY SPIRIT AND HIS MIGHTY POWER

Be very careful, then, how you live—not as unwise but as wise, making the most of every opportunity, because the days are evil. Therefore do not be foolish, but understand what the Lord's will is. Do not get drunk on wine, which leads to debauchery. Instead, be filled with the Spirit, speaking to one another with psalms, hymns, and songs from the Spirit. Sing and make music from your heart to the Lord, always giving thanks to God the Father for everything, in the name of our Lord Jesus Christ. (Ephesians 5:15–20)

Finally, be strong . . . in his mighty power. (Ephesians 6:10)

S everal biographers of D. L. Moody relate an account of what became a significant turning point in his ministry for God. Moody had been preaching for several years and was in great demand as a speaker. He was the founder and leader of one of the fastest growing and most effective Sunday schools in Chicago.

His ministry attracted even the attention and curiosity of Abraham Lincoln, who insisted on visiting Mr. Moody's Sunday school during one of his visits to Chicago. Moody's influence and ministry were reaching out farther and farther, but he had an area of weakness that needed recognition.

Following one of Mr. Moody's evangelistic meetings, two ladies lingered behind to speak to him. "We have been praying for you," they said, implying that they saw a need for prayer concerning his life and ministry.

That bold statement disturbed Moody. "Why don't you pray for the people?" he asked rather abruptly.

"Because you need the power of the Holy Spirit," they responded.

Ruffled, Moody responded, "I need the power?"

But those two ladies took the assignment from the Lord to pray that Mr. Moody be endued with the Holy Spirit's power. They were frequently in the front rows of his meetings, obviously much in prayer. At first Mr. Moody responded with annoyance, but his sincere heart soon began to respond in a positive way. Before long, the cry of his own heart was to be endued with the Spirit's power. He would frequently gather a group for a half day of prayer and would "groan and weep before God" for the Spirit's enduement.[1]

Then something unique happened in a hotel room in New York City. The authorized biography of Moody by William Moody, his son, quotes the evangelist as saying:

I was crying all the time that God would fill me with His Spirit. Well, one day, in the city of New York—oh, what a day! I cannot describe it, I seldom refer to it; it is almost too sacred an experience to name: Paul had an experience of which he never spoke for fourteen years.

I can only say that God revealed Himself to me, and I had such an experience of His love that I had to ask Him to stay His

hand. I went to preaching again. The sermons were not different. I did not present any new truths, and yet hundreds were
converted. I would not now be placed back where I was before
that blessed experience if you should give me all the world, it
would be as the small dust of the balance.[2]

Another biographer states, "God seems to have answered in
a mighty way the prayers of these two women, for at this time
his life changed considerably from that of a young, somewhat
cocky and proud preacher, to a humble, soft and mellow-
hearted preacher, who quietly, but richly, revealed . . . the compelling teaching of God's great love for men everywhere, as it is
revealed in the Bible."[3]

Giving the Person and work of the Holy Spirit place in his life
effected profound changes in Mr. Moody's ministry. He found
new power and effectiveness in snatching people from Satan's
bondage. Walter Knight writes of the subsequent effectiveness of
one of Moody's meetings in London. He preached to five thousand people, many of whom were professed atheists, agnostics,
and free-thinkers. Unbelief was so much in vogue in that day that
special clubs were organized all over London to foster fellowship
among those who had rejected the faith. They came to Moody's
meeting with cynical minds and scornful looks. Moody was
tempted to be intimidated by these learned, scornful skeptics,
but instead he claimed the mighty power of the Holy Spirit. He
preached the Word of God with great fervency and conviction.
Knight quotes Moody's own evaluation of the results:

In an instant, the Holy Spirit moved upon those enemies of Jesus
Christ. More than five-hundred of them stood. Tearfully they
cried out, "I will! I will come to Christ!" Quickly the meeting was
closed for personal work to begin. From that night until the end

of the week nearly two thousand men were won from the ranks of Satan into the army of the Lord. The enduring character of what took place was evidenced by the discontinuance of their atheistic clubs![4]

D. L. Moody became one of Christendom's most powerful proponents of the necessity of the Person and work of the Holy Spirit in believers' lives. He knew how dramatic could be one's victory over sin and Satan when filled with the Spirit's mighty power. He carefully avoided the excesses that have sometimes characterized emphasis upon the Holy Spirit's ministry. Yet, Mr. Moody was always ready to proclaim the truth that believers must be filled with the Spirit. The thousands upon thousands won to Christ during his evangelistic preaching resulted from the Spirit's empowerment. The revival meetings that sometimes went on for weeks with Mr. Moody preaching nightly also witness of that power.

Being filled with the Holy Spirit's power remains at the heart of all spiritual victory and Christian service. The great importance the Scripture assigns to the doctrine of the Holy Spirit is doubtless the reason there is so much confusion among believers about this subject. Both rational intellectualism and excessive emotionalism have tended to rob Christians of the marvelous ministry of the Holy Spirit in their lives. The kingdom of darkness is doing all that it can to keep the Holy Spirit's Person and work shut away from our practical usage.

A BALANCED PERSPECTIVE OF THE SPIRIT'S FILLING

On one hand, Christians face the problem of excessive emotionalism surrounding the Person of the Holy Spirit. This emphasis too often stresses experience and spiritistic manifestations into which demonic powers are always ready to intrude. Dr.

Merrill Unger in his book *What Demons Can Do to Saints* has documented several such cases.

Yet there is another side as well. Dead, cold, unbiblical intellectualism concerning the Person and work of the Holy Spirit gives Satan equal advantage against us. So called "institutional Christianity" has come under criticism in recent years. When religious worship is reduced to lifeless, impersonal ceremony, it is no wonder that people look elsewhere for their joys of life. Satan's program looks very appealing in contrast to the drab institutionalism that often makes up modern worship.

Nearly all the serious errors that have divided and hindered the Christian church have somehow been related to a lack of balance. There are many apparently paradoxical truths in Scripture that require balanced understanding. The sovereignty of God and the free will of man are a case in point. Predestination and the doctrine of election are thrilling truths. Yet, if we ignore the Bible's teaching on man's opportunity for choice and responsibility for decision, we will inevitably wander into trouble. The Word of God puts equal emphasis on both teachings.

Similarly, balance is the key to recognizing the work of the Holy Spirit in effecting victory. The Holy Spirit's ministry toward believers as set forth in God's Word has at least seven aspects. Balance is required to keep those ministries in proper perspective. Excessive emphasis upon one of the Spirit's ministries at the expense of the others begins to destroy balance. The enemy gets us preoccupied with tangents that rob our time and distract us from understanding the whole of the Spirit's work. As we daily appropriate the Holy Spirit's power, it is helpful to keep in mind the Spirit's seven unique ministries.

The Spirit's Convicting Ministry

But very truly I tell you, it is for your good that I am going away.
Unless I go away, the Advocate will not come to you; but if I go,

*I will send him to you. When he comes, he will prove the world
to be in the wrong about sin and righteousness and judgment:
about sin, because people do not believe in me; about righteousness, because I am going to the Father, where you can see
me no longer; and about judgment, because the prince of this
world now stands condemned.* (John 16:7–11)

The convicting ministry of the Holy Spirit expresses itself in
our lives even before we come to know Jesus Christ as our Lord
and Savior. The Lord Jesus told the grumbling Jews, "No one can
come to me unless the Father who sent me draws him. And I will
raise him up on the last day" (John 6:44 ESV).

The heavenly Father draws us by His Holy Spirit, convicting us of our sin, of God's righteousness, and of the certainty of
judgment to come. Though I was only eight when I converted to
Christ, the convicting work of the Holy Spirit is still vivid in my
memory. I knew I was sinful and needed to be saved.

On the day of Pentecost, after the Holy Spirit came and Peter
had preached his sermon, the conviction of the Holy Spirit was
present in power. "When the people heard this, they were cut to
the heart and said to Peter and the other apostles, 'Brothers, what
shall we do?'" (Acts 2:37).

The Holy Spirit takes God's Word and applies it to human
hearts. Guilt for sin, the righteousness of God, and accountability deserving judgment are brought to the human heart by the
Holy Spirit. That is how unbelievers come to know Christ as Lord
and Savior. This ministry of the Spirit is constantly active in our
world.

There is a sense in which the Holy Spirit also brings conviction upon believers if they have unconfessed sin in their lives. It
is a different kind of conviction, however. It comes as the wooing,
loving appeal of our heavenly Father to His children. It does not
center upon judgment and wrath but rather upon broken fel-

lowship and the need for restored relationship (see 1 John 1 and Hebrews 12:1–15).

Unfortunately, much so-called conviction in the lives of believers is really false guilt that is thrust upon them by the "accuser of the brethren." Revelation anticipates that day when

> "the accuser of our brethren has been thrown down, he who accuses them before our God day and night. And they overcame him because of the blood of the Lamb and because of the word of their testimony, and they did not love their life even when faced with death" (Revelation 12:10b–11 NASB).

We must understand the work of Satan's kingdom, or we may tragically attribute to the Holy Spirit what is really Satan's doing. Few believers escape Satan's clever ways of heaping guilt and self-condemnation upon themselves. He and his workers try to destroy a believer's sense of self-worth with accusations. "Look at you," comes the taunt. "You claim to be a Christian, yet you feel hate toward God and His Word. What kind of Christian are you? You deserve to be judged and go to hell." Such thoughts should be recognized as Satan's work. The Holy Spirit does not deal with believers that way. He may well reveal to us our acts of disobedience, but only to help us see the forgiveness and cleansing available through the blood of Christ. His purpose is to restore and assure us of God's love, forgiveness, and renewed fellowship.

One cannot warn too strongly of the importance of discerning the difference between the Holy Spirit's loving work toward believers and Satan's accusing, destroying actions. Consider the following comparisons:

The Holy Spirit's Work	**Satan's Work**
1. Seeks to show you that your worth and value to God make Him desire your fellowship.	1. Seeks to convince you that you are so bad that God wouldn't want to have anything to do with you.
2. Seeks to show you that there is forgiveness and restoration available no matter how bad your sin.	2. Seeks to convince you that there is no forgiveness for you, that you've committed the unpardonable sin.
3. Uses God's Word to give you hope and assurance of God's love and forgiveness.	3. Uses God's Word out of context to try to convince you that there is no hope for you.
4. Builds faith, hope, and love in your heart and increases your confidence and assurance of salvation.	4. Creates despair, doubt, resentment, and anger toward God, His Word, and His people. Tries to make you feel that no one as bad as you could ever really be saved.

False guilt is one of the most common maladies affecting believers today. Freedom from such guilt is exciting and life-giving.

A Christian engineer shared this testimony with me. It's the kind of testimony the Holy Spirit wants to give to every believer.

"You'll never know, pastor, what a life-transforming thing it has been for me to be free of false guilt. Ever since I was saved I've been haunted by my awareness of the sinful desires of my old nature. I'd feel so guilty and condemned when these desires would come to me. Now I see that these desires are just the expression of what God said my old sin nature is like. I am now able to reject them, and I seldom feel that destroying, paralyzing, self-condemning guilt anymore. If I do, I know how to fight it."

The Spirit's Indwelling Ministry

You, however, are not in the flesh but in the Spirit, if in fact the Spirit of God dwells in you. *Anyone who does not have the Spirit of Christ does not belong to him.* (Romans 8:9 ESV, emphasis added)

That text makes clear that the Holy Spirit comes to dwell within a believer at the moment of salvation. John 3:6 states, "Flesh gives birth to flesh, but the Spirit gives birth to spirit." At the moment of one's new birth, the Holy Spirit comes to dwell within the spirit of the believer. He is a literal presence, dwelling within the believer's body. "Do you not know that your bodies are temples of the Holy Spirit, who is in you, whom you have received from God?" (1 Corinthians 6:19).

Understanding that truth should protect us from some of the excesses of today's religious scene. We do not need more of the Holy Spirit. We have Him living, dwelling within our very beings. It remains for us to recognize His presence and to welcome His Person and work within us. We do not need more of Him; He needs more of us. We are to yield daily to His Person and His work within us. We will study that more as we consider the filling ministry of the Holy Spirit.

Recognizing and appropriating the Holy Spirit's indwelling presence has much to do with our success as Christians. Because He dwells within us, we can ask Him to daily produce within us the fruit of the Spirit. "But the fruit of the Spirit is love, joy, peace, forbearance, kindness, goodness, faithfulness, gentleness and self-control. Against such things there is no law" (Galatians 5:22–23).

The producing of that fruit does not require some new, super experience with the Holy Spirit. It is a matter of faith practiced on a daily basis. As the old nature tries to rule by causing us to manifest some of its expressions as set forth in Galatians 5:19–21, it is our responsibility to affirm that we are dead to its rule and then ask the Holy Spirit to produce His fruitful work within us.

The indwelling of the Holy Spirit is also the reason we can expect to understand God's Word as we read and study it. However, as it is written:

"What no eye has seen, nor ear heard, nor the heart of man imagined, what God has prepared for those who love him" —these things God has revealed to us through the Spirit. For the Spirit searches everything, even the depths of God. For who knows a person's thoughts except the spirit of that person, which is in him? So also no one comprehends the thoughts of God except the Spirit of God. Now we have received not the spirit of the world, but the Spirit who is from God, that we might understand the things freely given us by God. (1 Corinthians 2:9–12 ESV)

That aspect of the Holy Spirit's activity toward believers is often called His illuminating work. As we depend upon the indwelling Spirit of God when we study the Bible, He will bring its truth into our understanding. That is why it is so important to ask the Holy Spirit to illumine God's truth as we study or memorize it.

Many benefits flow from the indwelling work of the Holy Spirit. He is able to sanctify us, to keep us growing in grace, to give us His peace, and to enable us to practice love. Through His indwelling presence, He distributes the spiritual gifts He wants each believer to have (Romans 12:1–8; 1 Corinthians 12; Ephesians 4:7–13).

The Spirit's Baptizing Ministry

Just as a body, though one, has many parts, but all its many parts form one body, so it is with Christ. For we were all baptized by one Spirit so as to form one body—whether Jews or

Gentiles, slave or free—and we were all given the one Spirit to drink. (1 Corinthians 12:12–13)

The baptism "in the Holy Spirit," or "with the Holy Spirit," or "by the Holy Spirit" is a doctrine often disagreed upon by various Christian groups. Some insist that this work comes after salvation and is accompanied by speaking in tongues. First Corinthians 12:13 describes baptism by the Spirit as a work of the Holy Spirit that places all believers into Christ's body. His body is described in Ephesians 5:22–23 as His church. The Holy Spirit baptizes every believer at the moment of conversion into the Body of Christ, the body of all true believers. Just as a profession of faith and water baptism seem to have been the two requirements for entrance into the *local church* of the New Testament, so the new birth, accompanied by Holy Spirit baptism, is the means by which God puts us into the Body of Christ. Though our conversion may well be accompanied by joyful feelings, the baptism by the Spirit does not necessitate some experiential "high." Like justification, it takes place apart from experience. It's a marvelous comfort to realize that I do not need to seek and groan and strive to be baptized by the Holy Spirit. That work of the Holy Spirit unites us to the Lord Jesus Christ and to other believers as soon we believe.

The Spirit's Sealing Ministry

And you also were included in Christ when you heard the message of truth, the gospel of your salvation. When you believed, you were marked in him with a seal, the promised Holy Spirit, who is a deposit guaranteeing our inheritance until the redemption of those who are God's possession—to the praise of his glory. (Ephesians 1:13–14)

And do not grieve the Holy Spirit of God, with whom you were sealed for the day of redemption. (Ephesians 4:30)

Now it is God who makes both us and you stand firm in Christ. He anointed us, set his seal of ownership on us, and put his Spirit in our hearts as a deposit, guaranteeing what is to come.
(2 Corinthians 1:21–22)

Those texts make clear that sealing is a work of God, apart from any effort or striving on our part. We are sealed unto God the moment we are saved.

The sealing work of the Holy Spirit guarantees your security and assurance of eternal life. Satan and his kingdom will ceaselessly challenge your assurance of salvation. He will assert that you are not good enough to make it to heaven. What indescribable comfort and ceaseless praise should come to us in knowing that the seal of ownership is God's doing. It is the Holy Spirit who seals us until the day of redemption, guaranteeing what is to come.

> What indescribable comfort and ceaseless praise should come to us in knowing that the seal of ownership is God's doing.

The believer's security centers in the Trinity:

- The Father holds us in His grasp: "My Father, who has given them to me, is greater than all; no one can snatch them out of my Father's hand" (John 10:29).
- The Son secures us: "My sheep listen to my voice; I know them, and they follow me. I give them eternal life, and they shall never perish; no one will snatch them out of my hand" (John 10:27–28).
- The Holy Spirit seals every believer (Ephesians 1:13; 4:30).

In my view, the security of the believer is one of the most important biblical doctrines. If we have an understanding of our security hidden deeply in our faith, not even Satan himself can convince us to doubt.

The Spirit's Quickening Ministry

And if the Spirit of him who raised Jesus from the dead is living in you, he who raised Christ from the dead will also give life to your mortal bodies because of his Spirit, who lives in you. (Romans 8:11)

But because of his great love for us, God, who is rich in mercy, made us alive [quickened] with Christ even when we were dead in transgressions—it is by grace you have been saved. (Ephesians 2:4–5)

Quickening means bringing the dead to life. The Holy Spirit does that for believers.

"As for you, you were dead in your transgressions and sins, in which you used to live when you followed the ways of this world and of the ruler of the kingdom of the air, the spirit who is now at work in those who are disobedient" (Ephesians 2:1–2).

This text makes clear that before God brought us to spiritual life through the quickening work of the Holy Spirit, the ruler of the kingdom of the air, Satan, had a terrible hold upon us. After the Holy Spirit brought spiritual life into us as believers, we were set free from Satan's rule.

The quickening work of the Holy Spirit has three phases to it:

1. We were quickened and brought to spiritual life by the Holy Spirit the day we first believed.

2. We are being quickened as we daily walk in the Spirit and experience His life-giving work (Galatians 5:16–26).

3. We will yet be quickened at the Lord's coming when the Holy Spirit accomplishes that glorifying work in our mortal bodies (Romans 8:11; see also 1 Corinthians 15:42–58; Philippians 3:21; 1 Thessalonians 4:13–18).

Our bodies need the quickening power of the Holy Spirit before they will be ready to enter the glory of heaven. In Romans 6, the apostle Paul calls the body "the body of sin." "For we know that our old self was crucified with him so that the *body of sin* might be rendered powerless, that we should no longer be slaves to sin because anyone who has died has been freed from sin" (Romans 6:6–7 ESV, italics added).

Verses like this indicate that the old nature still has the potential to rule over us through our human bodies, which have not yet been quickened and glorified. The body is in process of dying; death is upon it, but it will one day be quickened in resurrection power by the Holy Spirit. We will then have glorified, immortal bodies like the one Jesus Christ had when He arose from the grave. "But our citizenship is in heaven. And we eagerly await a Savior from there, the Lord Jesus Christ, who, by the power that enables him to bring everything under his control, will transform our lowly bodies so that they will be like his glorious body" (Philippians 3:20–21).

The Spirit's Interceding Ministry

In the same way, the Spirit helps us in our weakness. We do not know what we ought to pray for, but the Spirit himself intercedes for us with wordless groans. And he who searches our hearts knows the mind of the Spirit, because the Spirit intercedes for God's people in accordance with the will of God. (Romans 8:26–27)

And pray in the Spirit on all occasions with all kinds of prayers and requests. With this in mind, be alert and always keep on praying for all the Lord's people. (Ephesians 6:18)

But you, dear friends, by building yourselves up in your most holy faith and praying in the Holy Spirit, keep yourselves in God's love as you wait for the mercy of our Lord Jesus Christ to bring you to eternal life. (Jude 20–21)

Those texts remind us that we have help with our praying. The Holy Spirit enables us to "pray in the Holy Spirit." That means that He comes to our side and helps us frame our prayers. It also means that He prays for us when we may be completely silent but depending upon the Holy Spirit to bring our requests before the throne of grace with His deep groanings.

Surely every believer has experienced the frailty of humanity that is common to us all, a frailty that may make prayer difficult. Sometimes as we wait on the Holy Spirit, He will free our minds and lips to express our longings to God. At other times, we may just kneel before the Lord in silence knowing that the Holy Spirit is bringing our petitions before God.

To say that "praying in the Spirit" requires the use of an unknown tongue is not correct. Paul makes clear in 1 Corinthians 14:13–17 that praying in the Spirit includes the use of the mind. Paul's prayers for the Ephesians (Ephesians 1:15–22; 3:14–19) and the believers in Colosse and Philippi were prayers in the Spirit. To pray in the Spirit simply means that we are being enabled by the Holy Spirit's control to pray according to His Word and His will. He enables us to pray and intercede in ways that we could not without His help.

The Spirit's Filling Ministry

After they prayed, the place where they were meeting was

shaken. And they were all filled with the Holy Spirit and spoke the word of God boldly. (Acts 4:31)

Therefore do not be foolish, but understand what the Lord's will is. Do not get drunk on wine, which leads to debauchery. Instead, be filled with the Spirit. (Ephesians 5:17–18)

The filling of the Spirit allows the Holy Spirit to accomplish the things He entered our lives to do. Through the Holy Spirit's filling, believers are empowered increasingly to walk in victory over the world, the flesh, and the devil. As a result of the filling of the Spirit our lives will exhibit what Paul called "the fruit of the Spirit"—the qualities that characterized the life of our Lord Jesus Christ when He was on earth. The Holy Spirit's filling provides us with power for service and enables us to exercise our spiritual gifts.

It is important that as we seek to find our strength in "His mighty power," we remain balanced, seeing the whole scope of the Holy Spirit's Person and work.

THE BENEFITS OF THE SPIRIT'S FILLING

The filling of the Holy Spirit brings many benefits to the Christian walk.

An Inner Benefit

Do not get drunk on wine. . . . Instead, be filled with the Spirit, speaking to one another with psalms, hymns, and songs from the Spirit. Sing and make music from your heart to the Lord. (Ephesians 5:18–19)

Those words hint at some wonderful, inner, and very human benefits for the believer who is experiencing the filling of the Spirit. Bible expositors have often noted the contrast between the Spirit's filling and being drunk. Not only is the contrast stated directly in Ephesians 5:18, but the initial filling of the Holy Spirit recorded in Acts 2 was misunderstood as a state of drunkenness. "Some . . . made fun of them and said, 'They have had too much wine'" (Acts 2:13). Peter responded to their misunderstanding by saying, "These people are not drunk, as you suppose. It's only nine in the morning! No, this is what was spoken by the prophet Joel: 'In the last days, God says, I will pour out my Spirit on all people'" (Acts 2:15–17a).

There is a marvelous promise here for people who have tried to find their "kicks" through alcohol and drugs. Drunkenness and drug trips are illusionary experiences. They create a false euphoria that is out of touch with reality. A drunk person is controlled by a force that releases his inhibitions; his troubles seem to disappear; he gains a boldness that sometimes can be dangerous for those in close proximity. The tragedy is that the euphoria is only temporary. He often awakens from his "trip" to find out that his troubles have increased. Perhaps he's been arrested for drunk driving or his wife has left him. Paul warns that the euphoria produced by alcoholism produces destruction.

Believers have an alternative that is satisfying and not illusionary. It's real. The alternative is the filling of the Holy Spirit. When He is in control, the inner benefits of love, joy, and peace prevail (Galatians 5:22). As Ephesians 5:19 indicates, the Spirit-filled believer can make music in his heart to praise God. The result is an inner calm that brings rest in even the most trying circumstances.

I was once given a form of sodium pentothal as an anesthetic for surgery. I quickly lapsed into an unconscious state, but during my time in the recovery room I experienced the false euphoria that some seek through drugs or alcohol. Under the control of the drug, my mind and emotions enjoyed sublime ecstasy. I felt so comfortable, so at peace, it seemed I was floating in paradise itself. As time lapsed, however, my euphoria gave way to a sensation of pain and discomfort from the surgery. The euphoria was not real; it was only masking the real pain. Yet, the more I came to consciousness, the more quiet and at rest I felt in the Lord. Many had been praying for me, and the Holy Spirit filled me with a calmness and a joy that did not eliminate the pain but was there in the midst of it. That inner benefit needs no additional source other than the Holy Spirit Himself.

An Upward Benefit

Sing and make music from your heart to the Lord, always giving thanks to God the Father for everything, in the name of our Lord Jesus Christ. (Ephesians 5:19–20)

The filling of the Holy Spirit produces joyful worship. To obey these words we must be filled with the Holy Spirit. Music of praise and thankfulness to the heavenly Father flows naturally from the heart of the Spirit-filled person. When praise, worship, and thankfulness seem foreign to us, we may need a fresh filling of the Holy Spirit.

While I was pastoring in Chicago, a touch of revival visited two churches in Pekin, Illinois. A couple who had led in the revival awakenings that came to Regina, Saskatchewan, in the early seventies were holding meetings there. The meetings at one church became so crowded that they had to be moved to a larger building. The meetings lasted for several weeks, dramatically affecting the lives of hundreds of believers and bringing many to Christ.

Hearing what God was doing, my wife and I decided to visit. It was a unique experience to be a part of such a powerful visitation of the Holy Spirit. As believers got right with one another and with their Lord, they were experiencing a fresh filling of the Spirit. We shall never forget the singing, the praises to the Lord, the joy, and the seemingly timeless nature of the evening. The service lasted for nearly four hours, but when it concluded people still lingered. They did not want to go home. Such revival helps illustrate the upward benefit of the Spirit's filling ministry. It allows praise, thanksgiving, and worship to flow freely.

An Outward Benefit

The imperative to be filled with the Holy Spirit in Ephesians immediately precedes the portions of Scripture that deal with personal relationships. Relationships between husbands and wives, children and parents, and workers and employers as set forth in Ephesians 5:21–6:9 are possible only through the Holy Spirit's filling ministry. The Holy Spirit can enable human beings to manifest a servant's heart that will make home, family, and working relationships harmonious and Christ exalting. The Spirit-filled life also prepares the believer to claim victory over Satan and his kingdom (Ephesians 6:10–18). We shall study this in more detail in succeeding chapters.

THE BASICS OF THE SPIRIT'S FILLING

Be filled with the Spirit. (Ephesians 5:18)

What are the basic necessities for the spiritual condition the Bible calls being "filled with the Spirit"? What must we do to achieve it? How can the available, beneficial, Christ-exalting fullness of the Spirit be ours?

The Word of God keeps the formula simple. We are not talking about a condition available only to "super saints." God means the fullness of the Spirit to be a part of the normal, daily living of every believer. What does it take to know this aspect of invincible living?

Regeneration—Finding New Birth (John 3:1–16)

It seems wise to stress this basic point. There may be some reading these words who have never been born from above. If you were to die and stand before God and He were to say, "Why should I let you into My heaven?" would you know how to answer? Salvation—eternal life—is God's free gift to be received as your personal possession. It becomes yours the moment you reach out in faith and claim the finished work of the Lord Jesus Christ as payment for your sins.

> "He came to that which was his own, but his own did not receive him. Yet to all who did receive him, to those who believed in his name, he gave the right to become children of God—children born not of natural descent, nor of human decision or a husband's will, but born of God" (John 1:11–13).

While writing this book, I visited a businessman who had recently received Christ as his Savior. Don and his family had attended our church, though he was not a believer. Much prayer and work had been exerted by the church to win him to Christ. His wife had been praying for his salvation for seven years.

When they made plans to move to another state, we invited them to our home for a farewell dinner. During the course of the evening, Don and I had a chance to talk alone. I mentioned that many of his friends hoped he might come to know Jesus Christ as his Lord and Savior before he moved away. That opened the door for conversation about eternal things, and in a matter of a few minutes, Don was praying and inviting Jesus Christ into his life to be his personal Savior and Lord.

The change he experienced was instant and profound. He immediately shared the joy of his new life with his wife, who was in another room. The next Sunday while attending church and Sunday school, he remarked that it was like someone had just turned on the lights. For the first time he could hear spiritual truth and understand what was being said. Subsequent visits with him confirmed his continued growth. Regeneration had taken place. "Therefore, if anyone is in Christ, he is a new creation. The old has passed away; behold, the new has come" (2 Corinthians 5:17 ESV).

I was reminded again of how transformative it is to receive Christ and to have the Holy Spirit enter one's life. All spiritual victory begins here. If any reader has not yet settled the matter of personal salvation, you must do that now. Invincible living never results from self-effort or turning over a new leaf. Victory is receiving a new life through the regenerating work of the Holy Spirit.

Elimination—Grieving the Spirit

Do not quench the Spirit. (1 Thessalonians 5:19)

And do not grieve the Holy Spirit of God, with whom you were sealed for the day of redemption. (Ephesians 4:30)

In his *Systematic Theology*, Lewis Sperry Chafer devotes an entire volume to the Person and work of the Holy Spirit, with sixty-five pages addressing "Conditions Prerequisite to Filling." Nearly all of those pages are given to a study of how we grieve and quench the Holy Spirit. Dr. Chafer concludes that the filling of the Holy Spirit requires only three conditions:

1. "quench not the Spirit" (1 Thessalonians 5:19 KJV),
2. "grieve not the holy Spirit of God" (Ephesians 4:30 KJV), and
3. "walk in the Spirit" (Galatians 5:16 KJV).

Grieving the Spirit is the result of unconfessed sin in the believer's life. We are therefore confronted with a twofold problem: How can we keep from sinning, and how do we apply God's provided cure once sin has entered our lives? The Holy Spirit is present to help us with those two major problems. If we do not rely on His Person and work to overcome the sin problem, we grieve Him. When He is grieved we will not know the victory and joy of His filling. It is of vital importance that we handle our sin problem on the basis of God's Word. That which grieves the Holy Spirit is instantly removed through confession expressed by a contrite heart. The moment we become aware of any grieving or estrangement, we need to determine the cause and apply the remedy.

Dedication—Yielding to God

Quenching the Spirit refers to resisting or rejecting the will of God for one's life. Yielding to God's plan allows the Holy Spirit's filling to make us invincibly strong. Being invincible means having the capacity and power to do God's will.

Dedication involves yielding totally to God's purpose.

Therefore do not let sin reign in your mortal body so that you obey its evil desires. Do not offer any part of yourself to sin as an instrument of wickedness, but rather offer yourselves to God as those who have been brought from death to life; and offer every part of yourself to him as an instrument of righteousness. . . . I am using an example from everyday life because of your human limitations. Just as you used to offer yourselves as slaves to impurity and to ever-increasing wickedness, so now offer yourselves as slaves to righteousness leading to holiness. (Romans 6:12–13, 19)

The Holy Spirit's work is so different from that of the spirit beings over which Satan rules. Wicked spirits seek to rule our lives through subtle trickery (Ephesians 6:11) and coercive force (Ephesians 6:12). Satan desires to manipulate us and force us to accomplish his plans.

The Holy Spirit does not work this way. He respects our personal dignity and gently woos us to respond to God's will. He is not interested in coercing us, but desires that we be willing responders. We do not do God's will through our own strength but through the supernatural work of the Holy Spirit within us. We must, however, yield ourselves to the Holy Spirit, expecting Him to accomplish God's will in us and through us. "I appeal to you therefore, brothers, by the mercies of God, to present your bodies as a living sacrifice, holy and acceptable to God, which is your spiritual worship" (Romans 12:1 ESV).

We must yield to the Lord and His plan in every experience of life, even the hard and the painful ones.

One of the heartbreaking stories of the Old Testament tells of the time King David fled with his family from the insurrection mounted by his own son Absalom (2 Samuel 16). As David approached Bahurim, a man from Saul's clan by the name of Shimei began to throw stones at the king and his company.

As he hurled his rocks, Shimei also pronounced curses upon David.

> "Get out, get out, you murderer, you scoundrel! The Lord has repaid you for all the blood you shed in the household of Saul, in whose place you have reigned. The LORD has given the kingdom into the hands of your son Absalom. You have come to ruin because you are a murderer!" (2 Samuel 16:7–8).

One of David's military men, Abishai, asked for permission to put an end to this indignity: "Let me go over and cut off his head" (2 Samuel 16:9).

David's response to Abishai's request might be paraphrased

Yieldedness says, "Lord, I hear You in this battle. I want to profit from it. I yield to what You are teaching me."

like this: "Don't harm him. I hear God in his words. The Lord is speaking to me in all of these happenings."

What a lesson for all of us to learn about yielding to the Lord. Even in one of the most trying times in David's life, he recognized that God in His sovereignty wanted to use the experience for David's profit and His own glory.

Every battle Satan launches against us somehow fits into God's sovereign plan. Even as we resist and reject Satan's purpose in attacking us, we must yield to the lessons and purposes God has in allowing us to face the battle. Failure to seek the Lord's teaching inevitably prolongs the battle. Yieldedness says, "Lord, I hear You in this battle. I want to profit from it. I yield to what You are teaching me."

Continuation—Walking in the Spirit

Those who belong to Christ Jesus have crucified the flesh with its passions and desires. Since we live by the Spirit, let us keep in step with the Spirit. Let us not become conceited, provoking and envying each other. (Galatians 5:24–26)

To keep in step with the Spirit or to "walk in the Spirit" requires moment by moment dependence upon the Spirit. We seriously err when we think we walk in the Spirit by our own human effort. We need to maintain an attitude of confidence and expectation that He will make walking in the Spirit a reality for us. To "walk in the Spirit" means to depend completely upon the Spirit, realizing that He alone can and will guide and help us.

What a delight it is for a parent to watch his or her little child learn to walk. It's always a time of much trial and error. There are many falls and failures in the process of learning to walk physically. Yet, once the skill is learned, walking becomes a practice that is done without thought.

Walking in the Spirit has a similar pattern. When we first see the need and desire to do so, the steps may seem halting and difficult. We will find ourselves resorting to serving the Lord in our own efforts. Self-effort displaces grace. Yet, when we fall, there is always forgiveness and the privilege of starting over. As we become more accustomed to the Spirit-led walk, we will find ourselves looking to the Holy Spirit moment by moment in every experience.

As we learn to walk in the Spirit it is excellent to begin each day with a prayer of expectancy, expressing our desire to experience the Holy Spirit's leading and enabling in every moment of the day. It is also helpful to take stock in the evening as you think through the day prayerfully. Offer praise and thanksgiving for the successes realized through the Spirit's work in you. Confess and repent of the times you relied on your own effort. This is a process that will go on as long as you live. To walk in the Spirit requires daily practice.

A PRAYER FOR THE SPIRIT'S FILLING

Loving Heavenly Father, I approach You again through the Person and work of the Lord Jesus Christ. I desire to obey Your will by being invincibly strong through Your Holy Spirit's enabling power. I praise You for Your goodness in providing the Holy Spirit for my benefit and strengthening. Thank You for that day when the Holy Spirit convicted me of my need of Your salvation. I praise You that He enabled me to open my heart to the Lord Jesus Christ and Your saving grace. I welcome the Holy Spirit's indwelling presence. It is with expectancy that I receive His peace, His comfort, and His illumination of my mind enabling me to understand Your Word. I greatly rejoice in the security of His sealing work. I delight that by His baptizing work the Spirit has put me into the Body of Christ and united me inseparably with Him. I praise Your name that the Holy Spirit has brought me to spiritual life and that He will yet quicken my body at the resurrection day.

As I pray, I am increasingly conscious of my need of the Spirit's intercessions in me, through me, and for me. I pray that You will grant me the privilege of praying in the Spirit. May my thoughts and words be directed by Him. May He bring my petitions into Your presence with His perfect understanding of Your will.

I acknowledge Your plan and Your desire to fill me with Your Holy Spirit. Forgive me for grieving the Holy Spirit by my sinning. Enable me to appropriate more perfectly the victory You have provided for me to walk above sin and failure. Grant to me always the awareness of my sins that I might quickly confess them to You. I do not want to quench the Holy Spirit by any reluctance to submit fully to Your will and plan for my life.

Help me to see moment by moment those things You are teaching me about Yourself and Your will for my life. It is my constant desire to walk in the Spirit. I ask You to fill me with His power that You might be glorified through the invincible strength You provide me to do Your will. All of this I ask in the name of the Lord Jesus Christ for Your glory. Amen.

NOTES

1. William R. Moody, *Life of D. L. Moody* (New York: H. Fleming Revell Company, 1900.), 261.
2. Ibid., 149.
3. Harry J. Albus, *A Treasury of Dwight L. Moody* (Grand Rapids: Eerdmans, 1949), 35.
4. Walter B. Knight, *Knight's Illustrations for Today* (Chicago: Moody Press, 1970), 150.

PART III

THE WHOLE ARMOR OF GOD

Put on the full armor of God, so that you can
take your stand against the devil's schemes.

For our struggle is not against flesh and blood,
but against the rulers, against the authorities,
against the powers of this dark world and against the
spiritual forces of evil in the heavenly realms.

Therefore put on the full armor of God, so that when the
day of evil comes, you may be able to stand your ground,
and after you have done everything, to stand.

EPHESIANS 6:11–13

5

THE BELT
OF TRUTH

Stand firm then, with the belt of truth buckled around your waist. (Ephesians 6:14a)

I was standing in the cafeteria of a Christian school when a young lady approached me with some hesitancy. "Are you Pastor Mark Bubeck?" she asked. When I responded that I was, she proceeded to pull out from the stack of books she was carrying a well-worn copy of *The Adversary*. It was so tattered and worn I could scarcely believe it. "I carry this book everywhere I go," she said. "I just had to thank you for writing it. It has been a tremendous help to me."

She obviously had my attention. I asked her to tell me her story. She related that before her conversion she had been deeply involved in the occult world of séances, fortune telling, and witchcraft. Because of Satan's cruel hold upon her life, she began to suffer greatly, but through God's loving providence she found the only way out. She received the Lord Jesus Christ as her Savior and was born again into God's family. In time she heard God's call to Christian service and was preparing herself in Bible school for missionary work.

Ever since her conversion, but particularly after she began Bible school training, there were times when she experienced excruciating attacks from the powers of darkness that once controlled her. She related that when those attacks came, they were so fierce and sudden that they seemed to completely disarm her. They would set her reeling in such confusion and pain that she could not think what to do or say. But as each attack came on, she would gain the presence of mind to turn to one of the doctrinal prayers in *The Adversary* and verbalize the prayer in her mind, even if unable to read it aloud. As she would address the doctrinal prayer to her Lord and against the attack, she could break the attack. "These attacks are coming less and less frequently," she related. "I don't think it will be long now until that's all behind me."

A BRUTAL FOE

As I later reflected on that encounter, I could not but think how typical that situation was in illustrating the ruthless, cruel attack of Satan. There is significance to the first part of the believer's armor being "the belt of truth buckled around your waist." Satan is an enemy who is always ready to "hit below the belt." In the sport of boxing, or any other sport for that matter, the sense of decency and fair play outlaws hitting below the belt. If by accident an opponent happens to get the wind knocked out of him, it warrants a time out or even a penalty against the opponent who caused the injury. Most of us have had the wind knocked out of us at some point or other and remember how helpless it rendered us for a time. Only the most ruthless opponent would deliberately set out to hit below the belt.

That is the kind of foe we have. Satan makes his ways appealing to us. That is why so many get drawn into the world of spiritism. It promises the ability to know the future, special powers other people do not have, the ability to contact a dead loved one. The appeal of Satan's promises is one of the reasons people buy occult books and magazines, pornographic literature, and pseudo-religious literature full of the "things taught by of demons" (1 Timothy 4:1).

Satan makes it look appealing, but when he gets you coming his way, you begin to see how ruthless he is. "The way of the unfaithful leads to their destruction" (Proverbs 13:15). "She who lives in pleasure is dead while she lives" (1 Timothy 5:6 NKJV).

Believers need to know that they have a ruthless foe who hits below the belt. He will do all he can to double you over and then bludgeon your head with his destructive blows. If God has taught me anything about spiritual warfare, it is that Satan is terribly ruthless and cruel. Many of those who are deeply into the occult, if they survive, begin to search for some way out simply because their suffering is so great that they cannot endure it any longer.

I received a call from a young lady experiencing fierce emotional and physical suffering. She had drifted into the occult. She had used a Ouija board frequently, but when she received conflicting answers at different times, she sought out a fortune teller's counsel to help her find answers to her problems.

At first the fortune teller refused to read her palm. But she finally agreed to read tarot cards for her and proceeded to describe the girl's future. Suddenly in the midst of her procedures the fortune teller quit the process, pushed the cards aside, and said, "You shouldn't be doing this. I shouldn't be doing this." She then turned, took from a shelf a copy of *The Adversary*, and gave it to the girl. "Here's a book you need to read," she said. "You're getting into trouble you don't know anything about."

Because of that response the young woman later contacted me. One can only surmise the reason that fortune teller had a copy of such a book in her possession. I daresay it was because she herself was going through torment of soul. Perhaps a Christian had given her a copy to help her see a way out.

Many of those who enter into Satan's domain find the suffering they experience absolutely ruthless in its intensity. If he makes his own followers endure such suffering, how much more ruthless would he be against those who belong to Christ, if unprotected? He will destroy you if he can.

In the words of Martin Luther's hymn, "his craft and power are great, and, armed with cruel hate, on earth is not his equal." One secret of Satan's craft is his clever use of lies. In speaking of the devil's final end, Revelation 20:10 states: "And the devil, *who deceived them,* was thrown into the lake of burning sulfur, where the beast and the false prophet had been thrown" (italics added).

The ultimate tactic of Satan's strategy is to deceive people. The Lord Jesus Christ confirmed this in John 8:44 when in rebuking the unbelieving Pharisees He said, "You belong to your father, the devil, and you want to carry out your father's desires. He was a murderer from the beginning, not holding to the truth, for there is no truth in him. When he lies, he speaks his native language, for he is a liar and the father of lies."

Whenever we are under assault from Satan, we can be sure that the lie is present someplace. Perhaps we have been deceived, and we believe something that is not true. That is often the case. Satan's roarings convince believers that they are vulnerable instead of victorious, so they succumb to fear and doubt about their position of invincible strength through their union with Christ. They believe Satan's lie, and that is the way he gains more ground against them.

THE WEAPON OF TRUTH

There is no more important weapon than truth. We must ask the Lord daily to show us any ways we are being deceived by Satan's lies. It is also vital to ask the Lord to help us always to speak and live the truth. In warning us not to give the devil a foothold in our lives, the apostle Paul also admonishes us, "Therefore each of you must put off falsehood and speak truthfully to your neighbor, for we are all members of one body" (Ephesians 4:25).

Contrary to what most of us would like to admit, the sin of lying is quite common among Christian believers. It can be so subtle. Misleading statements, a deliberate attempt to leave a wrong impression, half truths, so-called "white lies," as well as outright lies are all part of Satan's tactics to gain a foothold against us.

For years, a devoted Christian man had struggled unsuccessfully with the sin of lying. Sometimes he told inconsequential lies in ordinary conversation by adding embellishments to his stories to make them sound better. Occasionally he would tell total fabrications as true happenings to make his conversation more interesting. Afterwards he would feel guilty and ask the Lord's forgiveness, but because of the circumstances, it was often impossible for him to go back and make things right with the people to whom he had lied. It had become such an ingrained habit that he would fall into the practice before he even realized he was doing it.

Finally, in desperate earnestness to be rid of this sinful habit, he began to ask the Lord to help him realize that he was about to tell a lie before he began. The Lord heard his prayer, and step-by-step he was able to put away the practice and to speak only the truth. It was a joy to his heart to be free of lying. In that victory he took from Satan a powerful foothold. Many of us see some degree of ourselves in the man's experience. It is God's revealed truth that defeats Satan, but giving in to deception of any kind gives our enemy an advantage against us.

FOUR STRONGHOLDS OF TRUTH

The Word of God sets forth four great strongholds of truth that are part of the belt of truth:

1. The Lord Jesus Christ is the Person of truth. Jesus answered, "I am the way and *the truth* and the life. No one comes to the Father except through me" (John 14:6, italics added).

"The Word became flesh and made his dwelling among us. We have seen his glory, the glory of the one and only Son, who came from the Father, full of grace and *truth*" (John 1:14, italics added).

Jesus Christ is the very embodiment of absolute truth. He is our ultimate and total protection from takeover by Satan and his kingdom. In warning the Roman believers to avoid the sinful entrapments of the world, the flesh, and the devil, the apostle Paul urged in Romans 13:14, "Rather, clothe yourselves with the Lord Jesus Christ, and do not think about how to gratify the desires of the flesh."

As we study the armor of God, it is not surprising to see that each part of the armor is intimately related to the Person and work of Christ. As we put on the armor, we are in reality clothing ourselves with the protection of the Lord Jesus Christ.

Before his conversion, John had been deeply entrapped in drug usage. He had then gotten involved in Eastern mysticism. From there he had gone into witchcraft and the open worship of Satan. Through the patient, loving witness of one of his friends who had become a Christian, with painful difficulty he had come to know Christ as his personal Lord and Savior. Those who get deeply involved in Satan's realm do not easily get free enough to even comprehend the way of salvation. His conversion was an example of God's loving grace.

After his conversion, as is so often the case, Satan attacked him with devastating physical and emotional assault. In these attacks, he would find himself virtually paralyzed from head to foot. Once he was unable to speak or move, Satan would torment him with thoughts like: "You belong to us. We're going to kill you. You'll never be free. You'll never be able to work. You'd better give up. See how much power we have. This new faith will never work for you." This harassment would go on until he lost consciousness.

Victory didn't come until he began to fight back through his mind. Even though he could not speak or move, he could still think. Aggressively he would repeat these thoughts: *I put on the Lord Jesus Christ. He is the truth. Satan, you are a liar. In the name of the Lord Jesus Christ, I command you to release my body. I give my body only to the control of the Lord Jesus Christ, and I cover myself with the shelter of His precious blood.* As he applied the truth against the enemy, he could always break the attacking power and in moments be free from the immediate attack. Applied truth protected and delivered him.

> Each part of the armor is intimately related to the Person and work of Christ. As we put on the armor, we are in reality clothing ourselves with the protection of the Lord Jesus Christ.

Such an extreme case reminds us that even Satan's most powerful attacks are no match for the One who is the truth. Yet, the belt of truth is something each believer must put on by his own aggressive act. D. M. Lloyd Jones in his book *The Christian Soldier* states it this way:

> The Authorized Version translation in this instance is not as good as it might be; it is misleading in the sense that it puts it in a passive way instead of an active manner. Instead of reading, "Stand therefore, having your loins girt about with truth," as if someone else did it for you, a better translation is, "Stand therefore, having girded your loins with truth." In other words, it is we who have to do this. The girdle is not put on us, we have to put it on; and we have to put it firmly in position.[1]

Objective truth must be subjectively appropriated. That is why the young man mentioned above, when under fierce attack, had to aggressively fight back with his mind to claim and apply his victory. Victorious warfare requires action on our end. We cannot be passive, hoping someone else will act for us.

2. *The Word of God is the word of truth.* One argument for the inerrancy of Scripture is its own often-repeated claim to be the "word of truth." In 2 Timothy 2:15 we read, "Do your best to present yourself to God as one approved, a worker who does not need to be ashamed and who correctly handles the *word of truth*" (italics added).

James reminds us, "He chose to give us birth through the *word of truth*, that we might be a kind of firstfruits of all he created" (James 1:18, italics added). The psalmist prays, "Then I can answer anyone who taunts me, for I trust in your word. Never take your word of truth from my mouth, for I have put my hope in your laws" (Psalm 119:42–43).

It is difficult to count the number of times by direct statement or by implication the Bible claims to be the word of truth. The Bible is the final authority for truth in our world today. The troubles of our own personal lives, the troubles of the church, and most of the troubles of the world are due to a departure from the authority of the Bible as our only infallible standard for truth. Successful spiritual warfare begins with the ultimate question: Do I accept the Bible as the word of truth, the very Word of God, as the sole and final authority of what is true and what is error? Do I accept Scripture as God's revelation?

Before we can succeed in putting on the belt of truth, we have to come to God's Word with the faith of a little child and look to God to receive His divine revelation from the Word. We have to see that "the world through its wisdom did not know him [God]" (1 Corinthians 1:21), and never could. We can never trust man's wisdom and ability to reason to find truth. Truth comes by God's revelation. This is how we know where we stand; it is written in the Word. The word of truth, the Bible, is what we use to fight the enemy. This is how we deal with temptation and judge what is sin; the Bible reveals it. This is how we face the future with confidence; we have the word of truth—God's Word—unfolding a future of total victory in Christ.

3. *The Holy Spirit is the Spirit of truth.* The Holy Spirit is the One who illumines and opens the Word of truth to our understanding and profit. This is made clear in 1 Corinthians 2:6–15, which states that left to ourselves apart from the Spirit we could never understand the Word of truth since we do not have the Spirit of truth to illumine the Word to our spiritual understanding.

> *The Spirit searches all things, even the deep things of God. For who knows a person's thoughts except their own spirit within them? In the same way no one knows the thoughts of God except the Spirit of God. What we have received is not the spirit of the world, but the Spirit who is from God, so that we may understand what God has freely given us. This is what we speak, not in words taught us by human wisdom, but in words taught by the Spirit, explaining spiritual realities with Spirit-taught words. The person without the Spirit does not accept the things that come from the Spirit of God but considers them foolishness, and cannot understand them because they are discerned only through the Spirit.* (1 Corinthians 2:10–14)

There are some important practical truths to remember as we ask the Holy Spirit to reveal God's truth to us. First, we must know that the Holy Spirit will always lead us into beliefs, actions, and attitudes that accord with the Word of truth (the Bible) and the Person of truth (the Lord Jesus Christ). In this day of emphasis upon experience and the so-called charismatic gifts, that point needs to be carefully stressed. Those who look for extrabiblical revelations from the Holy Spirit and accept them as truth subject themselves to serious error.

I recently learned of a "spiritual leader" who stated that the Holy Spirit had revealed to her that she should divorce her husband so she would be free to give her full time to serving the Lord in her meetings. That does not fit with passages like Ephesians 5 and Titus 2:4–5. The Holy Spirit does not lead us to violate His inspired Word.

A man attending a church I once pastored declared that the Holy Spirit had given him the gift of prophecy. He seemed most radiant with his new gift and appeared to be walking in the joy of the Lord. The problem was that his prophecies contradicted God's Word at times. He was being deceived by his prophecies.

Second Peter 1:20–21 states,

> "Above all, you must understand that no prophecy of Scripture came about by the prophet's own interpretation of things. For prophecy never had its origin in the human will, but prophets, though human, spoke from God as they were carried along by the Holy Spirit." The Holy Spirit is the author of the Word of truth, and He certainly will never tell us to believe or do something contrary to the Word of God, although the subtle deceptions of Satan might lead us to believe otherwise.

How important it is to ask the Holy Spirit to guide us into truth as we read God's Word. The truth of our Lord and the truth of His Word will always protect us. Ask the Holy Spirit to protect you from being drawn into movements or emphases that are inconsistent with His truth. As we claim the Spirit of truth to protect us daily, He will do so, because that is His ministry.

4. The church is the pillar and foundation of truth. The apostle Paul in instructing Timothy stated, "Although I hope to come to you soon, I am writing you these instructions so that, if I am delayed, you will know how people ought to conduct themselves in God's household, which is the church of the living God, the pillar and foundation of the truth" (1 Timothy 3:14–15).

The local church is here raised to a high level of importance in God's plan. A local church is called "God's household" and "the church of the living God." Every believer is always to be related closely to a sound, Bible-centered, Christ-exalting local church. We are to submit ourselves to the disciplines, the checks and balances, that God in His sovereignty builds into the local church. Many times in my own personal life, even as a pastor, the Lord has used the ministry of the church to protect me from some sad error. How many times I have seen the ministry of the local church protect a believer from total defeat. When believers rally to pray, protect, and encourage, the enemy is put to flight. Affiliate with a local church, submit to its disciplines, attend the services, and be instructed in the Word.

Satan hates to face the believer who has the belt of truth buckled around their waist. Have you ever told a lie convincingly and then suddenly the truth came out? There you were, caught in your lie, absolutely devastated. The belt of truth affects Satan and his kingdom in the same way. It devastates and totally defeats him. It exposes his deceiving, lying ways for what they are and breaks his power against you.

How do we aggressively stand firm with the belt of truth buckled around our waist? It is done by prayer. The following prayer is designed to guide you in claiming a vital part of the armor.

A PRAYER TO PUT ON THE BELT OF TRUTH

In the name of the Lord Jesus Christ I claim the protection of the belt of truth, having buckled it securely around my waist. I pray the protection of the belt of truth over my personal life, my home and family, and the ministry God has appointed for my life. I use the belt of truth directly against Satan and his kingdom of darkness. I aggressively embrace Him who is the truth, the Lord Jesus Christ, as my strength and protection from all of Satan's deceptions. I desire that the truth of God's Word shall constantly gain a deeper place in my life. I pray that studying and memorizing the truth of God's Word may be my heart's delight.

Forgive me for my sin of not speaking the truth. Show me any way in which I am being deceived. By the Holy Spirit of truth, open the Scriptures to my understanding and guide me into the practical understanding of His words of truth. I ask the Holy Spirit to warn me before I deceive anyone and to ever protect me from believing Satan's lies. Thank You, Lord, for making my local church a pillar and foundation for Your truth in my life. Help me to relate to my church and to give protection and help to others as well as receive it myself.

I see, Lord Jesus Christ, that my ability to be invincibly strong and able to do Your will despite Satan's subtle ways requires the stabilizing power of the belt of truth. Thank You for providing this part of the armor. I accept it gratefully and desire to have an ever-deepening understanding of its protection through Your power. Amen.

Notes

1. D. M. Lloyd Jones, *The Christian Soldier* (Grand Rapids: Baker Book House, n.d.), 184.

6

THE BREASTPLATE OF RIGHTEOUSNESS

. . . with the breastplate of righteousness in place.
(Ephesians 6:14b)

The L<small>ORD</small> looked and was displeased that there was no justice. He saw that there was no one, he was appalled that there was no one to intervene; so his own arm achieved salvation for him, and his own righteousness sustained him. He put on righteousness as his breastplate, and the helmet of salvation on his head. (Isaiah 59:15b–17a)

Warren Wiersbe's book *The Strategy of Satan* tells of a little known character in the Old Testament, Joshua the high priest. Joshua was one of four people in the Old Testament who had a direct encounter with Satan (Zechariah 3). The story is illuminating because it shows how Satan goes for the heart of a man, the place where he is most vulnerable—where his conscience, or sense of rightness, resides.

The heart is a part of each of us that is often subject to defeat. One reason for that is our awareness of our failures, sins, and transgressions. If we do not feel guilty for sins of commission, we certainly know that we are guilty of sins of omission. Who of us can claim to meet God's standard, loving Him with all of the heart and mind and soul? Who of us ever comes close to always loving our neighbor as ourself?

Then there are the other sins of omission so common to God's own people: neglect of prayer, careless attention to the study of God's Word, lost opportunities for witnessing to friends and fellow workers, or forgetting to pray for someone we promised to remember.

The target of Satan against Joshua the high priest was his heart, his conscience, that part of him capable of responding to God, wanting to please God. The chapter opens with Joshua standing before the angel of the Lord and Satan standing "at his right side to accuse him" (Zechariah 3:1). Satan's weapon was accusation; his plan was to indict Joshua before the Lord. Satan wants to destroy the heart of the man. Accusing men as they approach God is another of Satan's effective weapons against believers. Our failures provide him with much ammunition.

In Revelation 12 a loud voice heralds the devil being thrown out of heaven. "The accuser of our brothers and sisters, who accuses them before our God day and night, has been hurled down" (Revelation 12:10). Satan accuses people. He accuses them before God day and night. Have you not heard him doing that to you? "How can you expect any help from God? Look at all of those sins you've committed. Look at how you've failed to do what you know you should."

On and on he goes. He wants to destroy your heart. He wants to convince you that you are such a failure that there is no use in going on. "How can God ever use such a bungling Christian as you?" More sincere Christians are defeated right here than perhaps at any other point.

The breastplate of a suit of armor is designed to protect an area of extreme vulnerability—the heart. In Zechariah 3, as Joshua the high priest is under severe attack and accusation by Satan, the Lord Himself comes to Joshua's rescue: "The LORD rebuke you, Satan! The LORD, who has chosen Jerusalem, rebuke you! Is not this man a burning stick snatched from the fire?" (Zechariah 3:2).

Joshua stands before the Lord dressed in "filthy clothes," representing Joshua's righteousness. Similarly, Isaiah 64:6 says, "All our righteous acts are like filthy rags." The angel says to those near Joshua, "Take off his filthy clothes" (Zechariah 3:4). Once that is done, the angel assures Joshua, "See, I have taken away your sin, and I will put fine garments on you" (Zechariah 3:4).

At the Lord's direction, Joshua is clothed in clean, pure garments and is thus fit to stand in the Lord's presence. He is then instructed to walk in those clean new garments in the strength and victory of the Lord. By so doing he will be a symbol of the coming servant of the Lord, the Branch, our Messiah (see Zechariah 3:6–10).

That Old Testament story is a fitting illustration of the part of the armor now before us. The breastplate of righteousness is the only protection we have against Satan's attack on the very heart of God's servants. The Roman soldier's breastplate was of unique importance in his armor, covering his body's most vulnerable organs: his heart, lungs, stomach, liver, and bowels. A wound by the enemy's sword, spear, or arrow in any one of those organs meant almost certain death. For that reason, the breastplate had to be incredibly strong and always in place.

Righteousness is thus given a place of unusual importance in the believer's warfare. There are several reasons this is so.

Righteousness defeats Satan. Righteousness defeats Satan —absolutely. Righteousness is all that Satan is not. He is unrighteous, wicked, evil, full of darkness (see John 8:44; 13:2; 1 John 3:8). Righteousness defeats Satan and turns him back. Why exactly?

Righteousness is one of God's attributes. The Psalms are filled with such statements as, "Your right hand is filled with righteousness" (48:10), "You are righteous, LORD" (119:137), "The LORD is righteous in all his ways" (145:17), and in Jeremiah, "And this is the name by which he will be called: *The LORD is our Righteousness*" (Jeremiah 23:6 ESV, italics added).What is the breastplate of righteousness? It is the Lord's righteousness bestowed upon us and in us that protects us.

Righteousness is imputed to us. "Imputed righteousness" means that when I am saved, God justifies me. God the Father puts the very righteousness of the Lord Jesus to my account; it is imputed to me, put upon me by God as a judicial act. God now looks at me as being clothed in His own righteousness.

In Philippians 3:8–9, the apostle Paul rejoices in this righteousness:

> "What is more, I consider everything a loss because of the surpassing worth of knowing Christ Jesus my Lord, for whose sake I have lost all things. I consider them garbage, that I may gain Christ and be found in him, not having a righteousness of my own that comes from the law, but that which is through faith in Christ—the righteousness that comes from God on the basis of faith."

Imputed righteousness means that something that belongs to one person (Christ) is accounted to another (the believer).

When we are justified, a marvelous exchange takes place. At the moment saving faith comes, God takes our sins *and* imputes them to Christ's account; they are seen as punished in Christ. At the same time, God also takes the righteousness of Christ and imputes it to us, and thus we are considered righteous.

Putting on the breastplate of righteousness means that we are daily refreshing ourselves with the awareness of that marvelous truth. Joshua the high priest was a picture of this truth. His own filthy garments were removed and new garments, clean and worthy for the Lord's presence, were put upon him.

There is no stronger protection against Satan's accusations about our unworthiness than to keep this truth of "imputed righteousness" ever before our minds. Romans 8:1–2 must become a conscious, daily certainty, "Therefore, there is now no condemnation for those who are in Christ Jesus, because through Christ Jesus the law of the Spirit who gives life has set you free from the law of sin and death." Satan will make no progress accusing us if that truth is hidden securely in our hearts and kept freshly before our minds.

Righteousness is imparted to us. God also imparts Christ's righteousness within us. The Puritans called this *imparted righteousness.* Imparted righteousness refers to the righteousness that God puts into my conduct and life. It is no less entirely from God than imputed righteousness, but it is in the realm of my experience and is not always constant and total. Sometimes I do sanctified, righteous deeds, but at other times I do not. Genuine righteous deeds result from God's action: "For it is God who works in you to will and to act in order to fulfill his good purpose" (Philippians 2:13).

In 1 Thessalonians 5:8 Paul instructs, "But since we belong to the day, let us be sober, putting on faith and love as a breastplate." A superficial study might cause us to conclude that this breastplate of faith and love is different from the breastplate of righteousness. Such is not the case. Faith and love are the very best expressions of the outworking of imparted righteousness. Faith and love are righteousness at work in the believer's life.

As we put on the breastplate of righteousness we need to appreciate the importance of both our imputed and imparted righteousness. God not only reckons us as righteous in His sight, but He also expects righteous deeds to flow from our lives. God's imputed righteousness is our breastplate of protection in the ultimate sense, but imparted righteousness is intended to flow from His investment.

THE BREASTPLATE'S PROTECTION

The breastplate of righteousness protects us in several ways. First, it helps give us confidence and courage. Few things are more essential to spiritual warfare than is assurance. When Satan throws his accusations against us, accusing us of our failures—which are only too obvious—it is heartening to know that it is Christ's imputed righteousness and not our own that makes us worthy. Confidence also comes from knowing that the imparted righteousness God planted in us can express itself in deeds of faith and love that glorify God, "and to put on the new self, created to be like God in true righteousness and holiness" (Ephesians 4:24).

A young man called me to express deep concern about his marriage. His young wife had shut him out of her life. She refused to seek counsel from anyone. She kept saying that the only solution to their problems was for him to leave. She suffered from a terrible inner anguish and torment, and found little rest. Both of these young people were Christians, but the distance between them had widened into a great breach. Their frustrations and anger had become so intense at times that they had actually struck each other. The accuser had also been busy in this trying relationship. The young man admitted that the call to me was a last ditch attempt on his part. Though involved in the Lord's work on a full-time basis, he was about ready to leave his wife.

As we discussed some practical steps he could take and talked about why he could be sure of victory in Christ, I could sense his confidence building. As we ended the conversation he was excited about beginning a time of fasting and prayer. Confidence and courage had increased as he "wore" his breastplate of righteousness. That is what the breastplate of righteousness is meant to do.

The breastplate of righteousness also allows us the opportunity to repudiate self-righteousness. As we daily claim the breastplate of righteousness we should renounce that ever-present tendency to pat ourselves on the back and say, "Look at how good I am."

Job had one of the most fearsome encounters with Satan recorded in the Word. One reason God allowed such a prolonged trial at Satan's instigation seems to have been to refine away Job's self-righteousness. As Job engaged in the early stages of dialogue with his friends, the idea that kept coming from him was, "I'm so good and right with God that I have no idea why God is allowing this terrible trial to occur in my life."

A young Christian woman in my church carried a despondent, somewhat angry look on her face for an extended period of time. I was thankful when one day she asked to have an appointment with me. As she began to share her burdens, she talked of some deep and distressing disappointments that had come into her life. They were hard blows that had upset her emotionally. She had allowed those disappointments to raise questions in her mind about the goodness of God. In a burst of tears she finally blurted out, "God has no right to treat me this way. I've always tried to put Him first and to keep my life free of sin. It's just not fair. It's just not fair."

As gently as I could, I tried to help her see that she was in essence saying, "God, You have no right to treat me this way, because I'm so good and so nice." When she saw this, she began to laugh and cry at the same time. Isaiah 64:6 lighted her path to repentance, "All of us have become like one who is unclean, and all our righteous acts are like filthy rags; we all shrivel up like a leaf, and like the wind our sins sweep us away." We talked about the fact that God's goodness is true whether or not our experience seems to testify to it. Goodness is the very essence of His character. When our experience does not seem to support that truth, we are to praise Him for His goodness anyway.

As the Lord revealed to her the self-righteousness of her heart, a beautiful prayer of repentance ensued. She left my presence that day with a look of radiant joy.

The breastplate of righteousness is meant to do that for every believer. It provides us the daily opportunity to remind ourselves that the only righteousness we have is that which our Lord imputes and imparts to us.

In times when God allows deep hurts and disappointments to come, we have the opportunity to receive them with joy. James instructs us to "count it all joy, my brothers, when you meet trials of various kinds, for you know that the testing of your faith produces steadfastness. And let steadfastness have its full effect, that you may be perfect and complete, lacking in nothing" (James 1:2–4 ESV).

If we find ourselves drawing back from the tests the Lord allows to come, it may be that a root of self-righteousness is present. We, too, are expressing the thought, "Lord, I'm too good to deserve this kind of treatment." We must praise the Lord even for the severities of the battle.

Trusting in self-goodness is not only worthless, but also makes us vulnerable to spiritual danger. By trusting in self-goodness, unbelievers are kept from saving faith. It is necessary to recognize one's utter sinfulness before the heart can be prepared for saving faith. In Romans, the apostle Paul draws from several Old Testament Scriptures to demonstrate to us our true condition.

What shall we conclude then? Do we have any advantage? Not at all! For we have already made the charge that Jews and Gentiles alike are all under the power of sin. As it is written: "There is no one righteous, not even one; there is no one who understands; there is no one who seeks God. All have turned away, they have together become worthless; there is no one who

does good, not even one." "Their throats are open graves; their
tongues practice deceit." "The poison of vipers is on their lips."
"Their mouths are full of cursing and bitterness." "Their feet
are swift to shed blood; ruin and misery mark their ways, and
the way of peace they do not know." "There is no fear of God
before their eyes." (Romans 3:9–18)

Those words should be sufficient cause for us to repudiate self-righteousness.

Trusting in self-goodness is no less worthless after we are saved. It is still an affront to God. God will never be able to use us effectively until we see that only His righteousness is worthy.

As Jesus lived on earth, one thing Satan could never touch was His righteousness.

Hebrews 4:15 declares, "For we do not have a high priest who is unable to empathize with our weaknesses, but we have one who has been tempted in every way, just as we are—yet he did not sin." Neither Satan nor sin could touch our Lord's righteousness. He was tempted, but temptation was always defeated.

It is important to remember that temptation is not sin. Some Christians get upset with themselves when temptation comes. I know of a man who almost wrecked his life over this point. He had lived a very sensual life before his conversion, and for a time after being saved the thought of anything immoral nauseated him. It was repulsive to him, and he was thankful for the evidence that "the old has gone, the new is here" (2 Corinthians 5:17). However, as time went on, old fleshly passions were occasionally stirred anew. He would walk by a book counter displaying pornographic reading material and be tempted to pick it up. These temptations greatly distressed him. He was sure they were a sign that he was about to return to his old ways. He reasoned that someone who has been saved and transformed should not have such temptations. He then began to think that if the thoughts were there, perhaps it would be no more evil to do the acts he once had done.

At that critical moment a Christian friend pointed out to him that temptation to do evil is not sin. Christ Himself was "tempted in every way, just as we are—yet he did not sin" (Hebrews 4:15). That knowledge comforted him greatly.

Temptation in and of itself does not soil righteousness. It is only when we entertain the temptation and lust after the object that sin invades our lives.

When we become believers, a threefold process of sanctification is set in motion:

First, in our position with God we are not only declared to be righteous but are also "set apart." That is called positional sanctification. The righteousness and holiness of Christ is credited to our account, and the Lord looks upon the believer as a "saint," even though in conduct he may not be very "saintly."

Second, sanctification is also a process that goes on throughout the believer's lifetime. As the apostle Paul closes his first letter to the Thessalonians he expresses the plea, "May God himself, the God of peace, sanctify you through and through. May your whole spirit, soul and body be kept blameless at the coming of our Lord Jesus Christ. The one who calls you is faithful, and he will do it" (1 Thessalonians 5:23–24). That process is sometimes called "growing in grace" and is carried on by assimilating God's Word into our lives through the agency of the Holy Spirit (Romans 15:16; 1 Corinthians 6:11; Philippians 2:12; 1 Timothy 4:7; 1 Peter 2:2).

The process of sanctification never ends or reaches perfection in this life. That is why we must claim the breastplate of righteousness on a daily basis. We all need to keep growing toward that measure of the stature of the fullness of Christ in our conduct (Ephesians 4:11–12; Colossians 3:5, 8, 12–14).

Third, our final sanctification will come when our Lord returns. First John 3:2b states, "But we know that when Christ appears, we shall be like him, for we shall see him as he is." At that moment, our sanctification in body, soul, and spirit will reach its total fulfillment. What God began at our conversion will be made complete.

The importance of putting on the breastplate of righteousness in an aggressive, active way cannot be over-stressed in spiritual warfare. The victory of our Lord's righteousness and the defeat it brings Satan and his kingdom must be aggressively applied and not passively assumed. This victory belongs to us, but we must lay hold of it.

THE DANGER OF PASSIVITY

I was seeking to motivate a Christian lady to active aggressive warfare. She had been in a fierce battle with Satan's kingdom for a number of years. Before becoming a Christian, she lived an extremely sinful life and had a background of occult practice. The harassment and suffering she endured from Satan had left her weary, worn, and feeling anything but aggressive.

Passiveness is always a dangerous state to be in when it comes to spiritual matters. "It's the Lord's battle," she said to me. "If I'm going to have victory in this fight, the Lord will have to do it."

We need to depend on the Lord for the ultimate victory, to be sure, but we also have to participate in the battle. We must not be totally passive.

Let us imagine that a soldier finds himself in the best-equipped army in the world. The latest weapons, the strongest armored tanks, and the most powerful rockets and bombs are at his disposal. But suppose that soldier goes out to face his enemy leaving his guns and other equipment behind. What will happen? Somebody with less equipment than he initially had can easily strike him down. He must use what has been given to him.

The application is obvious. We are members of God's army. We are to endure as good soldiers of Christ. We are equipped with all the armaments we need to defeat the enemy of our souls and his entire kingdom, but we must use them. The breastplate of righteousness is one of the most vital. We must claim its protection daily and aggressively use it to resist the devil and put him to flight.

A PRAYER TO PUT ON THE BREASTPLATE OF RIGHTEOUSNESS

In the name of the Lord Jesus Christ, I put on the breastplate of righteousness. In this moment, I repudiate any dependence I may have upon my own goodness. I embrace the righteousness that is mine by faith in the Lord Jesus Christ. I look to the Holy Spirit to be effecting righteous actions, pure thoughts, and holy attitudes in my life. I hold up the righteous life of the Lord Jesus Christ to defeat Satan and his kingdom. I affirm that my victory is won and lived out by my Savior. I eagerly ask and expect that the Lord Jesus Christ shall live His righteousness through me. Through the precious blood of Christ, cleanse me of all my sins of omission and commission. Let me walk in a holy and clean manner that honors God and defeats the world, the flesh, and the devil, through Jesus Christ my Lord. Amen.

7

THE SHOES
OF PEACE

*And with your feet fitted with the readiness that comes
from the gospel of peace.* (Ephesians 6:15)

*Peace I leave with you; my peace I give you. I do not
give to you as the world gives. Do not let your hearts be
troubled and do not be afraid.* (John 14:27)

Have you ever lost your sense of peace? What a time of panic, fear, and torment that brings. A dark time in my life still lurks in my consciousness as one of life's most fearsome moments. It happened in the early years of my marriage. I was in my second year of seminary, taking a full academic load, working part time, and struggling financially to make ends meet. There were some unresolved conflicts in my spiritual life, putting greater emotional and psychological pressure on me than I realized. Suddenly one day, as a result of a minor crisis, something snapped in my emotional well-being, and total panic swept in. Words fail to describe the darkness, the terror that comes to the human soul and spirit when fear begins to reign. Only those who have gone through such a valley will understand the hellish nature of the experience.

A similar experience happened to Charles Haddon Spurgeon following a speaking engagement at the Surrey Gardens Music Hall. As Spurgeon was speaking to an overflow crowd of more than 10,000 people, someone screamed "fire" and started a stampede for the exits. In the ensuing chaos, seven people were trampled to death and many others suffered serious injury. Mr. Spurgeon went into dark depression. He described the crisis:

> I refused to be comforted; tears were my meat by day, and dreams my terror by night. I felt as I had never felt before. "My thoughts were all a case of knives," cutting my heart in pieces until a kind of stupor of grief ministered a mournful medicine to me. I could have truly said, "I am not mad, but surely I have had enough to madden me, if I should indulge in meditation on it." I sought and found a solitude which seemed congenial to me. I could tell my griefs to the flowers, and the dews could weep with me. Here my mind lay, like a wreck upon the sand, incapable of its usual motion. I was in a strange land, and a stranger in it. My Bible, once my daily food, was but a hand to lift the sluices of my woe. Prayer yielded no balm to me; in fact, my soul was like an infant's soul, and I could not rise to the dignity of supplication. "Broken in pieces all asunder," my thoughts, which had been to me a cup of delights, were like pieces of broken glass, the piercing and cutting miseries of my pilgrimage.[1]

God's servants are not immune from such trials. Adding to my own trauma was the feeling of dread and humiliation that I was going to have a nervous breakdown. To me, that would be the worst thing that could possibly happen to a young man preparing for the ministry. *This can't be happening to me. I've never had a nervous day in my life. How can I ever be fit to comfort and counsel others in their spiritual and emotional needs when I've fallen apart?*

Thoughts like those were constantly with me. The only way to describe my torment during those days is to say that I was experiencing a total loss of my peace. My prayers, though fueled by desperation, seemed locked away from God's ears. The Scriptures, though often read, seemed like dead words to my troubled mind and emotions.

During those days, how thankful I was for a patient, prayerful, understanding wife and for Dr. Vernon Grounds, the godly president of the seminary I attended, who was a refuge of great comfort. As a trained psychologist, he was able to help me sort through some of the spiritual conflicts of my life. The trauma went on for several weeks, however, and seemed not to lessen in intensity. The extended time only added to my ultimate fear of having a total nervous collapse. How I longed for peace and wondered if it would ever return to my tormented life.

During that time, I learned that one of my professors had gone through a similar trial when he had been in seminary. Just knowing that someone else had experienced such a trial and survived comforted me. With a flicker of hope, I sought him out. He was most understanding and encouraging.

I expressed my fear of experiencing a nervous breakdown, perhaps ending my hope of ever being a minister. With kindness he spoke words that shocked me into a sudden awareness of truth. He said, "Mark, if God wants you to go through a nervous breakdown, you ought to want to have a nervous breakdown more than anything else in the world."

Those words stopped me. I did not hear anything else that was said. Truth had slain my pride and fear.

Excusing myself hurriedly, I made my way home to get alone with God. On the way, I remembered having prayed during a special prayer day at seminary, "Lord, while I'm in seminary, do in my life whatever You see needs doing to prepare me to be a usable servant." Those words now rushed back to my consciousness with new insight into what my trauma was all about.

I knelt in prayer that afternoon and, for the first time since the trauma began, felt I could commune with God. With quiet surrender I prayed, "Lord, You know I've feared and fought even the thought of having a nervous breakdown. I've not even considered that it might be in Your will to train and discipline me. Forgive me for my self-will and obstinate pride. Lord, You know I really don't want to go through a nervous collapse, but if You want me to, then here we go. I'm ready." At that moment I was sure that God was going to take me through such a breakdown, but instead, as I arose from my knees, I noticed the return of at least a portion of inner peace. As I continued to surrender to the Lord's perfect will, that peace kept growing. In a few weeks I was fully recovered.

What great lessons that experience taught me. During that traumatic time, God built within me a tenderness and an understanding for people going through emotional crisis that I would never have learned otherwise. He taught me the absolute necessity of full surrender to His will, even if it threatens my own desires. But perhaps the greatest lesson of all was to learn the value of peace.

Through the apostle Paul, the Holy Spirit describes peace as the shoes of the soldier in warfare. Shoes are indispensable to the soldier's armor. Have you noticed that if your feet hurt, you hurt all over? A severe corn on the little toe or a troublesome bunion can hurt so much that you just can't walk anymore, let alone fight. Likewise, in spiritual battle, if you are hurting, you are not going to be an effective soldier.

Good shoes are necessary for good footing. A Roman soldier with sword in hand needed to have shoes that gave him traction, stability, and sure footing. He could not fight a battle if his feet were easily knocked from under him. Again the application to spiritual warfare is obvious. If our shoes of peace are not secure and well-fitted, we will not long endure the battle the enemy presses against us.

A soldier's shoes give him ease of movement so he will be ready to meet any challenge. In life we need different kinds of shoes for different kinds of activity. The track runner needs light, well spiked track shoes to move rapidly over the cinders. The basketball player needs shoes with specially-designed soles to keep his feet from sliding on the polished boards. The construction worker would probably soon injure his feet if he wore dress shoes while guiding his jackhammer.

Similarly, we need a certain kind of shoes for spiritual battle. The only shoes that will see us to victory are the shoes of peace, and these have some important characteristics that must be understood and faithfully claimed by the invincible servant of the Lord.

POSITIONAL PEACE

Romans 5:1 declares, "Therefore, since we have been justified through faith, *we have peace with God* through our Lord Jesus Christ" (italics added). This kind of peace is not subjective, experiential peace, but objective and legal. The only way you gain this peace is to know it in your mind and receive it by faith. Through God's decree of justification, you have peace with God. That means God is not angry with you anymore. The war between God and the believer has ended.

Many years ago I heard a pastor preach on the subject of justification. He likened the word *therefore* to God's finger pointing back to the cross and the perfect work of redemption accomplished there. Therefore, because of the cross, because of what God did there to satisfy His own anger against sin, because of the full price Christ paid to take away all of our sin, because God reconciled the believing sinner to Himself, we are justified. Justification includes not only the removal of all of our sin but also the imputation of all the righteousness of Christ Himself. We are robed in His righteousness. Therefore, because God, in His own work and plan, has justified us, we have *peace with God.*

Peace with God is meant to bring peace to the believer's intellect and mind. Justification is not an experiential, feeling-based truth. The only way believers know we are justified—declared righteous in God's sight—is because God says so and we believe Him. Inner peace comes when we accept the plain fact of what God has done. As a result, we have peace with Him.

An incident comes to mind out of the life of a young friend. He was going through several trials. Discouraged because of the prolonged nature of the testings, he said to me one day, "I guess God is punishing me for something. I don't know why He's angry at me, but if He wants to be angry that's okay because He does everything well."

My young friend's attitude was commendable, but his theology was terrible. God does not pour His anger upon His own children. He does not inflict punitive hurt upon us. Yes, the Lord chastens or disciplines His own to correct them, but He does not judge or punish His servants. The punishment of sin was settled at the cross of Christ. Now all believers are justified. As a result, we all have peace with God.

Knowing and living in the reality of this truth is so important to being invincible in warfare. The mind needs to lay hold of this great truth. We must walk in the shoes of peace with God. If the soldier is always ill at ease with the thought that God may be angry with him or that he has to toe the mark to keep God's anger away, he will make a poor soldier.

EXPERIENTIAL PEACE

Philippians 4:6–7 reads, "Do not be anxious about anything, but in every situation, by prayer and petition, with thanksgiving, present your requests to God. And *the peace of God*, which transcends all understanding, will guard your hearts and your minds in Christ Jesus" (italics added).

If peace *with* God is an intellectual peace, the peace *of* God is an emotional, experiential peace. We can know all the facts about God's provisions, but if emotions do not support our knowledge, we will not be able to act upon what we know to be true.

The peace of God applies a balm of inner serenity to our emotions. If you have the peace of God, you feel at peace in mind and heart—the total inner person. All of us know what it is like to lack inner peace. Some crisis comes into our lives—some worry, some danger—and a turbulent storm rages within. Many people seek peace through tranquilizers, depressants, and other drugs. Others turn to illicit drugs or alcohol. Some try pseudo-religious movements such as transcendental meditation to find a solution for their lack of peace.

GOD'S PRESCRIBED TRANQUILIZER

How does the believer walk in the shoes of peace? Philippians 4:6–7 reminds us that it is through prayer. Time alone with God in thankful, prayerful petition is the most effective inner tranquilizer. No solution to inner disquiet is as effective as prayer. It always works. "Do not be anxious about anything," the imperative commands us. The peace of God transcends all understanding, and it is more than we really need to see us through. It is an overflow.

The next time you sense a great inner shaking or even just a slight inner disquiet, try prayer. Shut yourself away for thirty minutes or an hour to be alone with God. Use doctrinal praying. Pray back to God the truth of being "in Christ," inseparably united to Christ in all of His Person and work.

Pray through your understanding from the Word of the Person and work of the Holy Spirit. Pray on each part of the believer's armor. Thank the Lord for all of His grace and goodness. Tell Him about your anxieties and concerns. God will intervene to change things. It may be so gradual you will scarcely know how or when it happens, but when you finish you will discover the peace of God within your emotions. A quiet inner serenity and calm reigns even though the storm may still rage about you. I know that to be true both by experience and by the truth of God's Word. In fact, if you are practicing this kind of praying regularly, you will discover the peace of God is already there when the crisis happens.

Years ago I sensed the Lord calling me to a special time of fasting and prayer. Not knowing the Lord's purpose, I determined to fast for three days. When fasting, I usually try to set aside the times I usually would be eating to pray.

At the close of the second day, at the dinner hour, I had just finished a time of prayer when my wife called me to the phone. It was a long distance call from my oldest brother, informing me that both of my elderly parents had been killed in a single car accident. For a moment there was the stunned disbelief such news would bring to anyone, but suddenly I was aware of an inner peace that passed all understanding. The peace of God was already there like a reservoir of supply to keep my heart and mind stable through that trial. That peace was so great that I was able to bring a devotional message at my parents' funeral.

Scripture is utterly practical. When we lay hold of its promises, it helps us navigate every circumstance of life.

Have you ever considered that your lack of inner peace may be God's way of calling you to prayer? We have many marvelous electronic gadgets available to us today. One that was most fascinating when I wrote this book was that little "beeper" radio that many doctors, businessmen, and even pastors carried to enable people to signal them no matter where they were. Several doctors in the church I pastored kept their beepers with them when they came to church. Sometimes while we were at worship, a beeper would sound and the doctor signaled would quietly get up and leave.

A lack of inner peace could be God's beeper signal to you. God may be calling you for an audience with Himself. He wants fellowship with you, and in the process He will restore to you that peace that transcends all understanding.

PEACE THAT PROTECTS

Philippians 4:9 states; "Whatever you have learned or received or heard from me, or seen in me—put it into practice. And *the God of peace* will be with you" (italics added).

I recall hearing a gifted Bible teacher tell an experience that has left a great truth lingering with me. It seems his young son was having difficulty with a bully who would pick on him as he went to school. The boy talked it over with his father, and they decided the best course of action would be just to ignore the bully. Yet that seemed only to make the bully more bold. Every day as the boy walked to school the bully would tease and shove him, laughing at him for being too much of a coward to fight.

The boy and his father talked it over again and decided that maybe the best thing to do would be to accept the bully's challenge to fight. Even though the bully was bigger, perhaps when he saw that the little fellow had some fight in him, he would show his own cowardly streak. The problem got only worse, however, because the bully beat up the boy quite badly, and soon he was afraid to go to school.

Finally in desperation, the father decided he would just take his son by the hand and walk with him to school. An amazing thing happened. His little son, who was totally afraid to walk alone to school, put his hand in his father's hand and walked with his head held high. The bully was in his usual place ready to pounce on his victim, but ran away when he saw that six-foot dad. Without saying a word, the son looked at his father and smiled in relief. The bully never again gave him any trouble.

The bully we face, our enemy Satan, and his kingdom are too great for us to face alone, but when *the God of peace* is with us, we need not fear. As Paul closes the book of Romans, he states, "*The God of peace* will soon crush Satan under your feet" (Romans 16:20, italics added).

THE SECURITY OF OBEDIENCE

How do we maintain a walk in the shoes of peace? "When a man's ways please the Lord, he makes even his enemies to be at peace with him" (Proverbs 16:7 ESV). That proverb harmonizes with Philippians 4:9. Both texts stress obedience. As a believer seeks to walk in obedience to the Lord, the special protective presence of the God of peace abides with that believer. Disobedience will make us vulnerable to the attacks of Satan.

Lack of obedience in the life of King Saul was the reason God removed His protection from Saul and let him fall victim to his enemies. One instance is recounted in 1 Samuel 15, where Saul is said to have kept some of the animals of the Amalekites, which God had ordered Saul to utterly destroy. When Saul excused his lack of obedience by insisting that he only kept the animals to sacrifice them to God, Samuel's reply was devastating:

"Does the LORD delight in burnt offerings and sacrifices as much as in obeying the LORD? To obey is better than sacrifice, and to heed is better than the fat of rams. For rebellion is like the sin of divination, and arrogance like the evil of idolatry. Because you have rejected the word of the LORD, he has rejected you as king" (1 Samuel 15:22–23).

What important words for us. "These things happened to them as examples and were written down as warnings for us, on whom the culmination of the ages has come. So, if you think you are standing firm, be careful that you don't fall!" (1 Corinthians 10:11–12).

The presence of the God of peace with us to make us invincibly strong is related to walking in humble, dedicated obedience. Rebellion, disobedience to God's will, makes us vulnerable to defeat.

If you are resisting God's will, you must deal with that resistance. Defeat for you and victory for you r enemy will soon result unless the God of peace is put in control.

JESUS CHRIST—OUR PEACE

"But now in Christ Jesus you who once were far away have been brought near by the blood of Christ. For he himself is our peace" (Ephesians 2:13–14a). Our shoes of peace rest upon the relationship we have to the Person of peace. The Christian faith is not primarily a system of doctrines and dogmas that believers accept, though it certainly includes rich doctrine. The Christian faith is primarily a relationship with the Lord Jesus Christ, and "He himself is our peace."

Each part of the armor in its ultimate application remains the Person of Christ. When we walk in peace, we are walking in Him. Only in Him are we justified and do we have peace with God. It is in Christ that we are able to pray and receive answers that bring us the peace of God. Christ is the only one ever perfectly obedient to the God of peace. Our obedience is possible only because we are in Him. It is His perfect obedience that is credited to our account. As we by faith allow Him to live His life in us, experiential obedience in our lives glorifies Him.

There is nothing more foundational to successful warfare than having the right shoes—the shoes of peace—on our feet. Peace with God, the peace of God, the God of peace, and the Person of peace—the Lord Jesus Christ—are the essentials of shoes that enable us to firmly stand.

Satan's attempts to defeat us are seldom more obvious than when he attacks our sense of peace. His strategy is to create chaos within us. Those under satanic or demonic attack endure turmoil, disquiet, torment, and the lack of peace. The demonic man of Gadara described in Mark 5 is a tragic example of the extent to which Satan will rob people of peace.

Satan is also a false peacemaker. Satan and his kingdom offer pseudo-solutions for peace in abundance. Illicit drugs and alcohol addiction dull the human consciousness into a stupor of blissful peace, but when the effects wear off, the torment is so severe that one is driven again to seek relief through this false peace. Exotic religious systems abound today, promising their adherents a special peace if they will only follow these cults. For a time, false peace seems to work, but ultimate chaos is always near.

Those who followed Jim Jones and participated in his People's Temple cult told of the meetings over which Jones presided that were apparently so wonderfully warm and happy. One participant observed that while attending the meetings he "felt so good inside." But the feeling turned out to be Satan's false peace. History has never recorded a more discordant, terror-filled, notorious end to a cult than the murder-suicide deaths of more than 900 people in the jungle of Guyana. One of the army men who saw that awful scene in Jonestown observed, "There were no Bibles." That really tells the story. When people twist the Word of God or throw away the Word entirely, they throw away the only source of true peace by rejecting the Person of peace to whom Scripture testifies.

A PRAYER TO PUT ON THE SHOES OF PEACE

Loving Heavenly Father, by faith and in the name of the Lord Jesus Christ, I put on the shoes of peace. I accept Your declaration that I am justified and that I have peace with You. May my mind grasp that wondrous truth with ever increasing awareness. I thank You, Lord, that I need not carry any anxiety or suffer from inner torment or turmoil. Thank You, Lord Jesus, that You have invited me to make all of my needs known to You through prayer. Teach me to wait in Your presence until the inner peace of God, which transcends human understanding, replaces my anxiety. I desire to know the strong presence of Your peace. May You walk with me and say to me, "Don't be afraid; I will help you."

With all of my heart I want to be obedient to Your will at all times. May the fullness of Christ who is my peace enable me to so walk in Him so that the fullness of His peace may glorify God through me. I take the shoes of peace in the name of the Lord Jesus Christ, and by faith I shall walk in them this day. Amen.

NOTES

1. Charles H. Spurgeon, *Charles Haddon Spurgeon: Autobiography, Volume 2: The Full Harvest*, 1861–1892 (Carlisle, Pa.: Banner of Truth, 1975), 195–96.

8

THE SHIELD
OF FAITH

*In addition to all this, take up the shield of faith, with which
you can extinguish all the flaming arrows of the evil one.*
(Ephesians 6:16)

On our twenty-fifth wedding anniversary, my wife and I were
seated next to the plate glass window of the restaurant atop
the John Hancock Building in Chicago, then heralded as the
world's tallest building—when including the height of the an-
tenna. The shoreline of Lake Michigan stretched before our gaze
and combined with the majestic skyline of Chicago to make our
romantic evening even more delightful. As we relived our twenty-
five happy years together, we failed to notice an approaching thun-
derstorm. Suddenly we were jarred by a blast of lightning followed
almost instantaneously by a thunderous roar. Our table—in fact,
the entire restaurant—seemed to tremble. From the vantage point
of our window table, we watched the storm rage with startling
fury. The clouds were inky black. The rain swirled and churned
in the wind and seemed to burst against the glass in a fierce effort
to reach us. The flashing lightning and roaring thunder continued to add brilliant color and stereophonic sound to the drama

of shrieking wind and splashing rain. It was a bit unnerving for a time; then the thundershower passed as suddenly as it had come, and the setting sun returned to paint its glory on the departing clouds.

I have since reflected upon how that experience illustrates the shield of faith. We could see the storm, even feel something of its fury, but it could not reach us. We were shielded by heavy plate glass engineered to meet just such storms.

The shield of faith is an important part of the believer's armor. "In addition to all this," the text says, we are to take the "shield of faith." The importance of the shield is seen in the words "with which you can extinguish *all* the flaming arrows of the evil one" (italics added). That is about as inclusive as it can be. *All* of the blazing missiles of the kingdom of Satan can be extinguished, quenched, put out by the protection of the shield. From behind the shield, you can sometimes see Satan's arrows streaking toward you. You can sometimes hear the thunder of his roar and feel the trembling of his fury, but the shield is strong enough to endure Satan's rage.

SHIELDED IN EVERY DIRECTION

One reason the shield of faith is so critical to the believer's walk is that it provides *complete* protection. The Greek word for shield, *thureos,* conveys the idea of a large shield. You might picture it as a shield that thoroughly encapsulates you. Psalm 5:12 states, "Surely, Lord, you bless the righteous; you *surround* them with your favor as with a shield" (italics added). The psalmist saw God's shield literally surrounding the righteous, protecting them from all directions. The Lord's protection is in front of us, behind us, above us, beneath us, on our right hand, and on our left. God's shield provides thorough protection.

Many years ago we toured the Space Center Museum at Huntsville, Alabama. We were fortunate to have a dear friend, Alfred Finzel, escort us on the tour. Al, now deceased, was one of the German scientists who worked so successfully with Werner Von Braun in our country's space program. One of the fascinating exhibits of that museum features the space capsules of the various moon probes. The environment of space is so hostile to human life, the scorching heat of re-entry into the earth's atmosphere so intense, that no human life could survive without the "every direction shielding" of those space capsules. That pictures the believer's shield of faith. The hostile atmosphere of Satan's kingdom is too deadly for us to survive without the shield of faith.

Before he was allowed to tempt Job, Satan complained to God, "Have you not put a hedge around him and his household and everything he has?" (Job 1:10a). God's shield was there to protect Job from the hostile atmosphere of Satan's hate and rage. The story of Job proves that Satan would torment and kill all of the righteous if it were not for God's shielding. We shall have more to say later about how Satan's efforts were able to pass through that shield in some measure, and why, but at this point it is good to note how high and adequate was God's hedge.

THE OBJECT OF OUR FAITH

A further reason the shield is so critical to victory is seen in the object of our faith. Our faith is not our shield, but rather the object of our faith is our shield. Faith in itself can provide no protection if the object of the faith is faulty.

Some of us recall the civil war that raged in Zaire while it was still the Congo. Under Moise Tshombe, foreign mercenaries were hired to put down the rebellion. The professional, well-trained soldiers were more than a match for the poorly trained rebel Congolese soldiers. As they were pushed back farther and farther by the mercenaries, the rebels began to flee in fear. In desperation, the rebel leaders promoted a scheme. A witch doctor's concoction that looked like white ashes was to be spread all over the bodies of the rebel soldiers. They were assured that this concoction would shield them from the bullets of the mercenaries. Bravely, with complete faith in this new "magic shield," many of the rebels made a stand, sometimes exposing themselves openly to the mercenary marksmen. They were sure they would be shielded by the "magic ash," but of course they were soon shot down by their enemies' bullets. Their faith failed because the object of their faith had no power to shield them. Proverbs 30:5 states, "Every word of God is flawless; he is a shield to those who take refuge in him."

> Our faith is not our shield, but rather the object of our faith is our shield. Faith in itself can provide no protection if the object of the faith is faulty.

Faith is merely the means the believer has of appropriating the shield. God is the object of our faith. He is our shield.

CONFIDENCE IN THE SHIELD

A third reason the shield is critical to our victory is that it provides the believer with the *confidence* of protection. Does the presence of the shield mean that Satan will never be allowed to touch us? Some people think so. The story of Job should forever lay to rest such thoughts. Satan was allowed to get through to him. The believer has no assurance that he will not experience some of the same kinds of trials from Satan's kingdom.

How can we explain such happenings if the shield of faith is able to quench *all* of Satan's fiery darts?

The answer can be found only by carefully examining the sovereign workings of our Lord. Satan's blazing missiles are always intended to hurt and destroy the believer. He is absolutely ruthless and devastatingly cruel in his attacks.

A fine Christ-centered family wrote to me of their troubled college-age daughter. She showed evidence of being a dedicated believer in the Savior. Articulate and brilliant, on intelligence tests she scored near the genius level. Her future seemed bright until she was faced with Satan's challenge. Let me quote from her mother's letter:

> She began having very troubled nights and would often come running in terror to our bedroom, saying she had a nightmare and wanted to sleep on the floor of our bedroom. . . . She told us really hair-raising tales of nightly visits from Satan, who would taunt her and attempt to goad her into accepting both his physical "love" and his way of life. . . . She is now living with a sister, who has told us that she does not sleep at night anymore, but stays awake all night and then sleeps in the daytime. Until two weeks ago, she could not be alone in the evening or night, as her terror was unbearable. She told her sister that she was seeing not only Satan but many demons at night in her room. She said that these demons rushed around the corners of her room and crawled up her bedposts to peer into her face.

How hideous and tormenting Satan can be. In this girl's case, her Christian psychiatrist recognized that she "was having identity problems and also was experiencing demonic oppression." Satan's ultimate purpose is to destroy, to tear down, to afflict, to torment, and to kill us if God would permit. Concerning Job, God said to Satan: "Very well, then, he is in your hands; but you must spare his life" (Job 2:6). This leaves little doubt that apart from God's shield, Satan would have killed Job as he did Job's family.

THE LORD'S
PURPOSE IN BATTLE

But what of God's purpose, we must ask? That God some-times lets Satan afflict believers despite the shield of faith and the rest of the armor is obvious both in the Word of God and in life. What is God's purpose and what happens to Satan's missiles?

As Satan's fiery darts penetrate the shield of faith—if in God's sovereignty He allows them to do so—they cease to be Satan's flaming missiles. Rather, they become the refining and purifying messengers of God's love.

Fire can destroy, or it can refine. Some friends of mine had a fire hit their apartment building. The next morning I walked with my friend through the remains of his burned-out apartment to see if we could salvage anything. The destruction was terrible. Everything was burned. All of their lifetime keepsakes, all of their clothing was destroyed.

Yet fire can be purifying too. I recall as a youth melting down lead to be poured into various shapes and molds. I loved to get the torch so hot that the molten metal seemed transparent. The hotter it got, the more latent impurities would rise to the top and have to be skimmed off, always leaving the metal purer than it was before.

That is what God does when He lets some of Satan's fiery darts pass through His shield. Under His sovereign eye, God never lets Satan's work go any further than He intends. James 1:2–4 says, "Consider it pure joy, my brothers and sisters, whenever you face trials of many kinds, because you know that the testing of your faith produces perseverance. Let perseverance finish its work so that you may be mature and complete, not lacking anything." First Peter 1:6–7 states, "In all this you greatly rejoice, though now for a little while you may have had to suffer grief in all kinds of trials. These have come so that the proven genuineness of your faith— of greater worth than gold, which perishes even though refined by fire—may result in praise, glory and honor when Jesus Christ is revealed." Consider the assurance of 1 Corinthians 10:13: "No temptation has overtaken you except what is common to mankind. And God is faithful; he will not let you be tempted beyond what you can bear. But when you are tempted, he will also provide a way out so that you can endure it."

STAYING GOD-CENTERED

We must remain God-centered and never become Satan-centered. That is always a danger. We must not become so conscious of Satan's power that we are always "fighting the devil" instead of "serving the Lord."

Again, Job is a good example for us. All of Job's sufferings and problems were directly from Satan's hands. Yet, as Job discusses his torment with his three friends and even with the Lord, his thoughts, words, and hopes were God-centered. Job never even credited Satan with producing his affliction. He kept his eyes upon the Lord, and ultimate victory came.

When under Satan's attack—even while we are resisting him and his purposes—we need to be thanking God for His purposes in allowing the battle. Satan means to produce evil and hurt, but God purposes to refine the believer and make him a stronger servant. Through Jeremiah, the Lord said to Israel, "Like clay in the hand of the potter, so are you in my hand" (Jeremiah 18:6b). That is a biblical principle we must respect and never forget. Just as controlled fire is one of man's greatest assets, so the controlled fires of Satan's afflictions in God's hands are in our lives for good.

A pastor recently told me about his work with a woman who had experienced years of terrible satanic affliction. It extended back into her childhood. She remembered that uncontrollable rages would sweep over her at the most unexpected moments. In adulthood, the problems worsened. A difficult marriage, unfaithfulness that led to adultery, and the resulting guilt added to the problem. After her husband's death, desperate to find answers, she got involved rather deeply in spiritism. That involvement accelerated her difficulties with the world of demons.

Just entering the bathroom would trigger vulgar thoughts, and obscene language would pour from her mouth. Voices from the spirit world would ceaselessly torment her, demanding and cajoling her to certain actions. When the experiences had reached a zenith, the pastor came on the scene. The woman's first response was to avoid him at the prompting of the voices, but during a painful attack she finally turned to the pastor for help.

Not sure how to proceed, he spent considerable time seeking to lead her to Christ but encountered fierce opposition by the powers of darkness. As the way of salvation was explained to her, she found the harassing voices and confusion almost unbearable. She and the pastor could proceed only with much patience and prayer. Finally, a breakthrough came, and she was able to pray to receive Christ. Great relief and calm ensued but did not last long.

The pastor related that a copy of *The Adversary* had come into his hands, and with some believing friends he sought to free this suffering woman from her torments. They boldly encountered the enemy. Several demonic powers identified their presence and were commanded to leave. Several sessions of prolonged prayer and warfare were necessary, but today that woman is free, rejoicing in the Lord. Sometimes she can still hear voices, but they are far away and barely audible, as if a great shield is between her and their presence. Before they left, some threatened to return if she ever backslid and gave them a chance, but she is determined to memorize the Word and walk with her Lord. She has resolved to keep her mind centered upon the Lord and His Word, and not upon the enemy. That is one of the keys to continual victory. We must never become preoccupied with the enemy but instead be totally occupied with God and His Word.

THE DEADLY NATURE
OF THE BATTLE

We must recognize the deadly nature of the battle the believer is in. Various translators use graphic language to describe what Satan shoots at us. "Flaming arrows," "fiery darts," "blazing missiles" all convey the sneaky, deadly serious nature of the evil one's intent.

The tactic of using flaming arrows in warfare is almost as old as war itself. In the days of walled cities, if attacking troops could shoot enough flaming arrows over the walls to start fires, their battle was easier. If the troops inside the city were occupied with putting out fires, they would not be able to guard against the advancing troops. That is very similar to Satan's strategy against us. He likes nothing better than to keep us busy fighting fires rather than resisting him and keeping our attention upon our Savior. His purpose is not only to destroy, but to divert us, to create panic and terror. If he can get the city afire and divert our attention, he will then be able to walk in and take over.

The threat of fire is real to many who live in the beautiful canyons of southern California. That was particularly true in the late summer and fall of 1978 when we lived there. Heavy rains in the early spring had created a lush growth of grass and brush on all the hillsides. The dry summer months and the Santa Ana winds off the desert had made every canyon a potential firetrap. Terrible fires swept through several canyons, burning hundreds of beautiful homes in a few moments of time. The fierce heat caused almost everything in the path of the fire to explode. Yet, there were some homes that were spared, usually because the owners had devised a method of shielding their homes from the flames. One such homeowner had devised an extensive sprinkler system, driven by a gasoline powered pump that drew water from the family swimming pool. As the fires approached and the air was full of blazing missiles driven by the high winds, the sprinkler system was activated, thoroughly drenching the house, the roof, the bushes and trees, and the area around the home. The missiles were all quenched as they fell on the shield of water. Though every other house in that area was consumed, the one with the carefully prepared shield of water was untouched. Reading that account in the newspaper, I could not help but see the comparison to spiritual warfare. The presence of the shield does not stop the blazing missiles from being thrown, but it does ensure that no damage will result. All of the missiles are quenched.

APPROPRIATING THE SHIELD

Let us now consider what this shield is and how we can appropriate its protection. The shield of faith in its fullest meaning is the sovereign omnipresence of our triune God.

God made a promise to Abraham: "The word of the Lord came to Abram in a vision: 'Do not be afraid, Abram. I am your *shield*, your very great reward'" (Genesis 15:1, italics added).

Through Moses, God said to Israel, "Blessed are you, Israel! Who is like you, a people saved by the LORD? He is your *shield* and helper and your glorious sword. Your enemies will cower before you, and you will tread on their heights" (Deuteronomy 33:29, italics added).

In one of David's songs of praise he sang, "The LORD is my rock, my fortress and my deliverer; my God is my rock, in whom I take refuge, *my shield* and the horn of my salvation. . . . You make your saving help my *shield*; your help has made me great" (2 Samuel 22:2–3, 36, italics added). There are more than a dozen references in the Psalms to the Lord Himself as our shield.

Satan is a created being, unable to overcome the Person and presence of the Lord. It is of great comfort to know that our shield of faith is the formidable power and Person of the Lord Himself.

Through faith, we are aware of the presence of the Lord between us and the enemy. Notice that the shield is "the shield *of faith*" and that the text says, "With which *you* can extinguish all the flaming arrows of the evil one" (Ephesians 6:16, italics added). *You,* the believer, have something to do with the extinguishing of the flaming arrows, and the shield *of faith* requires our active faith for its effectiveness.

> The shield of faith in its fullest meaning is the sovereign omnipresence of our triune God.

We must actively participate in our warfare. The shield's protection is something we must take and use on a daily basis.

Some believers question the necessity of putting on each part of the armor daily. "Why should I so often go through an act of aggressively taking or claiming my armor? Won't it become a habit or 'vain repetition'?"

I often encounter such questions and remind those asking that none of us would think of not dressing daily simply because doing so is repetitious. We put on clothing because we do not want to be embarrassed by our nakedness as we go out to face the world. How much more we need spiritual dress. Much more is at stake than just embarrassment. We are in a war with a deadly enemy who will take advantage of missing armor.

You may say, "Well, why did the Lord plan it that way? Why didn't He provide me with armor that I don't have to claim on a daily basis?" The answer to that may be seen, in part, in God's provision of manna in the Old Testament. The Lord wanted the Israelites to gather it daily. Any excess gathered, except for use on the Sabbath, always spoiled. It had to be freshly gathered to sustain life and provide blessing. Each daily gathering reminded the people that it was from God; it was His provision, evidence of His goodness. Our Lord builds into all of His dealings with us provisions that require daily communion and daily appropriation of His grace. There may be times when we will put on each part with haste and slight thought. Yet, there will be other times when we carefully meditate upon the significance of each part of the armor, resulting in loving worship of our Lord.

GUARDIAN ANGELS

Angels exercise a much more important part in shielding us than most of us realize. Hebrews 1:14 states, "Are not all angels ministering spirits sent to serve those who will inherit salvation?"

The psalmist promised, "For he will command his angels concerning you to *guard* you in all your ways" (Psalm 91:11, italics added). In such texts the term *guardian angel* takes on relevant meaning.

The angels exercise a vital role in fulfilling God's sovereign plan to shield us from Satan's darts. As spirit beings, the holy angels are not limited to the physical world as we are. They see the fallen angels as they attack us and are able to advance against them.

A striking picture of the ministry of shielding angels is seen in the story of Elisha in 2 Kings. The king of Aram wanted to work his strategy against the king of Israel, but every time he made plans, the king of Israel knew about them and frustrated him. Furious, the king of Aram was sure that some of his own men were cooperating with the king of Israel. One of his officers replied, "None of us, my lord the king . . . but Elisha, the prophet who is in Israel, tells the king of Israel the very words you speak in your bedroom" (2 Kings 6:12).

Upon learning this, the king of Aram sent a strong contingent of armed and mounted troops to surround the city of Dothan and to capture and destroy Elisha.

The next morning when Elisha's servant saw the city surrounded he was exceedingly fearful, but when he told Elisha, the prophet was calm. "Don't be afraid," the prophet answered. "Those who are with us are more than those who are with them" (2 Kings 6:16).

Elisha asked the Lord to let his servant see the protection of the angelic host, and suddenly the servant saw the hills full of horse-drawn chariots of fire all about Elisha. As the enemy troops approached, they were stricken with blindness by the Lord's host and diverted away in defeat.

Angels are more active in our affairs than most of us ever realize. Hebrews 13:2 reminds us, "Do not forget to show hospitality to strangers, for by so doing some people have shown hospitality to angels without knowing it."

Angels entered into battle with the powers of darkness in Daniel 10. The holy angel who came to Daniel had met in combat a fallen angel called "the prince of the Persian kingdom." Even Michael, one of the chief holy angels, got involved, and reference is made to a further battle with the Prince of Persia and the Prince of Greece (Daniel 10:15–21). In taking your shield of faith, ask for the presence of the holy angels to protect you. Knowing that angels are in the hills about you as you face your enemy is very reassuring. Elisha was not in any more need of protection than we are. Anyone doing the Lord's business is a target for destruction.

THE BLOOD OF CHRIST

We must never forget that the blood of Jesus Christ is the basis for the believer's acceptance by our holy and righteous heavenly Father. "In him we have redemption through his blood, the forgiveness of sins, in accordance with the riches of God's grace. . . . But now in Christ Jesus you who once were far away have been brought near by the blood of Christ" (Ephesians 1:7; 2:13). Verses like these harmonize with 1 Peter 1:2, 19 and Hebrews 9:7–14 to establish that it is through the blood of Christ that God is able to accept us.

The blood of Christ has a powerful effect in defeating Satan. In Revelation 12:11, a loud voice from heaven proclaims Satan's defeat and the victory of the redeemed in these words: "They triumphed over him by the blood of the Lamb and by the word of their testimony; they did not love their lives so much as to shrink from death."

Christ's death through the shedding of His blood effectively shields us. Hebrews 2:14–15 states, "Since the children have flesh and blood, he too shared in their humanity so that by his death he might break the power of him who holds the power of death— that is, the devil—and free those who all their lives were held in slavery by their fear of death."

What a perfect and complete shield we have. It extinguishes all the flaming arrows of Satan, if we use it. Failure to use the shield will allow some of Satan's fiery darts to work against believers.

A PRAYER TO TAKE UP THE SHIELD

Loving Heavenly Father, by faith I take the protection of the shield of faith. I count upon Your holy presence to surround me like a capsule, offering total protection from all of Satan's flaming arrows. Grant me the grace to accept Your refining purpose in allowing any of Satan's arrows to pass through the shield, and even to praise You for it. Help me to concentrate upon Your presence and not the enemy's arrows.

In the name of the Lord Jesus Christ I claim the protection of the holy angels to guard and shield me from the assaults of Satan's kingdom. May these ministering angels be present to interfere with the strategy of Satan to harm me and my family. I appropriate the victory of the blood of the Lord Jesus Christ and hold it against the advances of the evil one. With gratitude and praise, in the name of the Lord Jesus Christ I rejoice in Your victory. Amen.

9

THE HELMET OF SALVATION

Take the helmet of salvation. (Ephesians 6:17a)

Do not conform to the pattern of this world, but be transformed by the renewing of your mind. Then you will be able to test and approve what God's will is—his good, pleasing and perfect will. (Romans 12:2)

In *The Strategy of Satan,* Warren Wiersbe relates the four times in the Old Testament when Satan directly approached people. The first study deals with the temptation of Eve in the Garden. The first strategy of Satan, as recorded in Genesis 3:1–7, was targeted upon Eve's mind. The apostle Paul sees this approach as one of Satan's chief tactics, stating, "But I am afraid that just as Eve was deceived by the serpent's cunning, your *minds* may somehow be led astray from your sincere and pure devotion to Christ" (2 Corinthians 11:3, italics added).

THE MIND UNDER SIEGE

Satan's target is our minds. His weapons are his subtle and clever lies (Genesis 3:1–7; John 8:44; Romans 1:25). His lies are so clever that we have little defense against them unless we soundly know the truth. Satan wants to keep us ignorant of God's truth so that he can control our minds.

A Canadian father with a broken heart came to see me. A man in his late sixties, he told me the sad story of his daughter.

In her youth and teen years, his daughter had been a brilliant student. She had captured most of the academic prizes throughout her years of formal education. Her skill at typing allowed her to come within a hair's breadth of setting a new world record for typing speed. She was full of happiness and had a zest for living that made her attractive to everyone.

But inside her heart was a void, an emptiness that she longed to fill. By his own admission, her father was at least an agnostic, if not an outright atheist. His marriage had ended in divorce, and close family ties were severely strained. With no spiritual values, his brilliant daughter began to search for something to fill the spiritual void.

She studied Eastern mysticism and became deeply involved in the Hare Krishna movement. She pursued transcendental meditation with evangelistic fervor for a time and married a man involved in the study of Eastern mysticism. Her five thousand dollar savings account was given to him so that he might go to India and study under a renowned teacher. Upon his return from that study, they both began to experiment with the occult, becoming involved in séances and other practices of witchcraft. When some frightening experiences with the spirit world began to plague her during this experimentation, she had a superficial Christian experience that she called being "born again." It seems certain that it was not the spiritual "rebirth" our Savior spoke about. The fruit of that experience was extreme fanaticism and continued sinful living.

Confusion began to rule her mind. She could not hold a job and was in and out of several mental hospitals. She and her husband lived together only sporadically. Her baby had to be taken from her because of her neglect, and she readily offered the child up for adoption. Though her brilliance was still obvious, her mind seemed not her own. Outside voices told her what to do, and her confusion left her a helpless soul, unstable and unable to function. The distraught father, still an unbeliever, asked if the church could be of any help to his daughter.

Cases like this one are multiplying in our time. I am presently working with at least a half dozen cases that are almost identical. Good minds, often brilliant minds, become hopelessly confused and disoriented. Too many times troubled ones are unwilling to seek help on their own. They cannot understand why anyone is upset by their erratic behavior. They just want to be left alone so that they can get on with their irresponsible living. When this happens, such individuals become a terrible burden to their families and to society.

The apostle Paul seems to have had such situations in mind when he told Timothy to "gently instruct" such people "in the hope that God will grant them repentance leading them to a knowledge of the truth, and that they will come to their senses and escape from the trap of the devil, who has taken them captive to do his will" (2 Timothy 2:25–26). The emphasis upon "gently instruct," "knowledge of the truth," and "come to their senses" seems to indicate that the problem is one of deception; they have believed something that is false to be true.

To bring back someone from such a state, first be sure that she is genuinely saved. Next, put her under the care of a well-grounded Christian. Systematic teaching of the truth of God from the Bible, memorization of large portions of the Word, and careful instruction in spiritual warfare are the three most important steps in helping a person to get free from such problems.

PROTECTING THE MIND

The head is one of the most vulnerable body parts. Soldiers are not the only ones who have to wear helmets. Construction workers, motorcycle riders, football players, and even baseball players when at bat wear protective helmets. If the head is severely injured, the rest of the body soon begins to malfunction.

Recently, a young man in our church was injured in an industrial accident. A heavy barrel fell forty feet, breaking his back in several places. Despite the severe injuries to his body, he probably would have recovered if not for the terrible injury to his brain. When the brain began to fail, it was not long until the rest of the body's organs began to fail and death ensued.

In spiritual matters, the same holds true. If Satan can capture the mind with his lies, he begins to control and destroy the whole person. If the mind goes, everything goes.

During my seminary days I worked in construction on a government project. One rule was firmly imposed: No one could be anyplace on that large construction project without wearing his helmet, and not wearing it was cause for immediate dismissal. With that same kind of urgency, the apostle Paul instructs us to wear our helmet of salvation.

Many biblical passages warn us that our minds are vulnerable to the subtle ways of Satan. James 1:8 warns that a "double-minded person" is "unstable in all they do." To be double-minded is to try to live with two minds. It is a kind of spiritual schizophrenia; the mind divides itself into two parts. One part believes truth, and the other part believes Satan's lies.

When David prayed, "Give me an undivided heart, that I may fear your name," he was showing his awareness of the problem of double-mindedness in spiritual matters (Psalm 86:11). We must also be aware of the tendency to have faith in some areas but not in others, to be willing to be victorious in some battles but not in others, to want to do God's will to a certain point but not beyond that.

SATAN'S STRATEGIES TO CONTROL THE MIND

Ephesians 2:2 makes clear that prior to our conversion we were under the control of "the ruler of the kingdom of the air, the spirit who is now at work in those who are disobedient." Colossians 1:21 tells us, "Once you were alienated from God and were enemies in your *minds* because of your evil behavior" (italics added). Romans 8:6–7 states, "The mind governed by the flesh is death, but the mind governed by the Spirit is life and peace. The mind governed by the flesh is hostile to God; it does not submit to God's law, nor can it do so."

If Satan cannot control all of your mind as a believer, he is quite content to take the part that you will let him have by being double-minded or by not keeping your thoughts captive to the truth.

Ananias and Sapphira were professing believers and a part of the early church. But they met with God's severest discipline, death, because, as Peter says, "Satan filled your heart to lie to the Holy Spirit" (Acts 5:3 ESV).

Satan tries to attack the mind of believers relentlessly and ruthlessly. He wants to use his power to project his thoughts into our minds so that we think his thoughts are our own. That was true of Ananias and Sapphira. They thought the scheme to keep part of the money for their property, while telling the disciples they were giving it all to the Lord, was their own idea, but it was not. It was part of Satan's lie and they believed it and acted upon it.

A Christian brother shared that he was troubled by thoughts that often came while he was praying. He would suddenly begin to think, "Pray to Satan! Pray to Satan!" He felt terrible guilt that such hideous thoughts could be in his mind. He was greatly relieved to see that the thoughts were projected into his mind by Satan's kingdom and he was not responsible for them. He was responsible only to resist and reject them and to command the powers of darkness to leave him, in Jesus' name, and to go where the Lord Jesus Christ would send them.

JESUS CHRIST
AS OUR HELMET

When the aged Simeon took the baby Jesus into his arms and praised God, one of his expressions of praise was: "My eyes have seen your salvation" (Luke 2:30). Salvation was a Person that Simeon could see and hold in his arms. The psalmist declared, "The LORD is my light and my salvation" (Psalm 27:1). Peter proclaimed, "Salvation is found in no one else" (Acts 4:12). Salvation is a Person more than a condition or a state of being.

A friend of mine has spent most of his life witnessing for Christ to Jewish people. If a Jewish person says to him, "The name Jesus isn't even once stated in the Old Testament as the name of Messiah," he delights in turning in the Hebrew Bible to a verse of Scripture that has the word *salvation* in it. If they know enough Hebrew, he asks them to pronounce the word *salvation* in Hebrew. The word is *shuah,* meaning "safety, deliverance, or salvation," and *shuah* is also part of the pronunciation for *Jesus* in Hebrew, which is *Yeshua.* Every time a Jew reads or utters the word *salvation* in Hebrew, he or she is anticipating the name *Jesus.* Joseph was told by the angel concerning the child to be born of Mary, "You are to give him the name Jesus, because he will save his people from their sins" (Matthew 1:21). He is our salvation; salvation is a Person.

True salvation requires someone else to rescue you from a situation in which you are helpless. When I was young, on a very hot summer day I went swimming with a number of my brothers and cousins in the local gravel pit. The water, though very cold near the bottom, was well-warmed by the sun on the surface and ideal for swimming. We decided to swim across the pit, a distance of fifty yards or so, to see who could make it the fastest. I was not then a competent swimmer, and when I started to fall behind and grow tired, I decided to turn back and swim to the starting point. But I was tiring very rapidly, and panic began to set in, adding to my fatigue. I wondered if I would make it. Finally, when my strength seemed drained, I thought I was near enough to the shore to quit swimming and walk on in. I put my feet down but could feel no ground. I went under. My feet finally hit bottom, and I pushed myself to the surface. With water in my lungs, too weak to swim, I was going under a second time when a man on the shore saw me. Quickly he stepped into the water, thrust out his strong hand toward me, and I grabbed it with all the strength I had left. He pulled me to shore, and I was saved. He was my salvation. There was no way I could have done one thing further to save myself. At that moment I needed a savior to prevent me from drowning.

That is true of everyone who is saved from sin. We were lost and undone. We were going down for the last time and could not do one thing to rescue ourselves. We needed salvation—a Person to reach out His nail-scarred hands and save us from perishing forever. That's what Jesus Christ did. He is our salvation.

After becoming believers, however, there are still areas in which we are helpless to save ourselves. One of those areas is our mind. We need the helmet of salvation to protect our minds from the projected thoughts and attitudes of Satan and his demon powers.

HOW THE HELMET PROTECTS

The best way to keep Satan's thoughts out is to keep Christ's thoughts in. As surely as Satan can "fill [our] hearts," so much more can the Lord Jesus fill our minds with His thoughts. Unlike Satan, however, the Lord Jesus does not intrude where He is not invited. That's why it is up to us to invite the Lord Jesus Christ to enable us to think His thoughts after Him. It is one of those responsibilities of grace that is our moment by moment duty. It is why we memorize God's Word. It is part of putting on the armor.

Throughout the day, then, one should be alert to maintain that stance of faith. The moment a thought comes to mind that we recognize to be of the flesh or of Satanic origin, it is good to say, "In the name of the Lord Jesus Christ I reject this thought as being wrong. I ask my Lord Jesus Christ to replace it with His thoughts."

There is no surer way of putting the mind of Christ within us than by putting His Word into our minds. We often say that Jesus Christ is the living Word of God and that the Bible is the written Word of God. Scripture offers a marvelous correlation between the Person of Christ and the Word of Christ.

When we memorize the Word of God, we actually put within our minds the mind of Christ. That Word becomes a helmet of salvation to the mind. David found that out long before Christ came to earth: "I have hidden your word in my heart that I might not sin against you" (Psalm 119:11). David was putting the mind of Christ within him even before the Person of Christ had been revealed through the incarnation. If you are serious about protecting your mind from Satan's control, you must fill it with God's Word.

Lester Roloff of Corpus Christi, Texas, had a remarkable ministry with delinquent boys and girls, drug addicts, and alcoholics. Many chaotic and broken lives came to order and healing through his homes. One key to his success was firm discipline administered in love. Residents had to comply with discipline: to avoid all substances that have a narcotic affect upon the body, to respect authority, to work and study, to worship and pray, and

THE HELMET OF SALVATION

most important to memorize the Word of God. They committed to memory entire chapters of Scripture. The lives that have been dramatically turned around through this ministry are a testimony to the importance of getting the Word into the mind. The power of God's Word is essential to spiritual warfare. Those tormented by Satan's attack upon their minds need God's Word in their minds. One of the most effective things you can do for someone so tormented is to help him memorize Scripture.

HOPE SHIELDS THE MIND

In 1 Thessalonians 5:8–9, the apostle Paul states, "But since we belong to the day, let us be sober, putting on faith and love as a breastplate, and the *hope* of salvation as a helmet. For God did not appoint us to suffer wrath but to receive salvation through our Lord Jesus Christ" (italics added). Here the helmet of salvation is described as the hope of salvation.

Have you ever been lost in a forest? It is a frightening experience. While on an elk hunting expedition, I once got lost for the better part of a day. As we left camp that morning, our guide pointed toward a basin several miles above timberline and explained that we would meet there sometime in the afternoon. If any of us got separated from his hunting partner, he was to head for that basin. He promised to meet us there and guide us back to camp.

We were instructed to keep a couple hundred yards between us so that we might better stumble onto an elk. But that made it difficult to keep one's hunting partner in view, and it was not long until my partner and I were separated. The forest was so vast I could no longer see that distant basin. On top of that, clouds covered the sun, and my sense of direction was gone. My only encouragement that I was going in the right direction was that I kept going uphill. After several hours of walking and climbing,

I was not interested so much in hunting as in just hoping that someone would find me. I did not have a clue as to how I would ever find my way back to camp.

Finally, I broke out above timberline, saw the basin, made my way there, and sat down on a large rock to wait. Several hours passed, but no hunters appeared. To add to my anxiety, the sky darkened and it began to snow lightly.

I am sure that at that moment I would have panicked if it had not been for one fact. I had hope that my guide would come for me. He had promised. He had told us where to wait. I was sure that I was at the only rocky basin in that whole area and, therefore, he must come even though it seemed past time for him to be there. The snow kept falling harder. I was feeling the cold and knew that if a heavy snow fell, I would be hopelessly lost and would probably die of exposure without help. It was hope that my guide would come that kept me confident.

Finally, late in the afternoon, far below, I could see a man climbing toward me. It was our guide. He had kept his word. The rest of the hunters had turned back because of the snow, but he had come on with my hunting partner to find me. I was so glad to see them. I had developed high altitude sickness from over-exertion and would never have walked out alone. By morning, more than two feet of snow had fallen on our camp, and we had to depart from the mountains before we were snowed in.

That experience helps to illustrate the hope of salvation. Christ is our salvation and our hope. He is coming to rescue us. At the moment of His return that will be true, but it is also true in every experience of the believer's life. Just when we feel the most lost and forsaken, just when the enemy seems to be winning the day, just when the storm is heaviest, the hope of salvation comes to lead us back to safety. If the helmet of salvation is covering our minds, we need never lose hope. We always know He is going to come. He knows where we are. "God has said, 'Never will I leave you; never will I forsake you.' So we say with confidence, 'The LORD is my helper; I will not be afraid. What can mere mortals do to me?'" (Hebrews 13:5–6).

The writer to the Hebrews asks a searching question of believers: "How shall we escape if we ignore so great a salvation? This salvation, which was first announced by the Lord, was confirmed to us by those who heard him" (Hebrews 2:3). That question is pertinent to spiritual warfare. God has provided the helmet of salvation; we must take it. We must not passively assume our salvation but aggressively *take* Him, His mind, His Word, His power, and His presence. The emphasis is not on being saved from our sins but rather on what is available to us since we have been saved. It is a salvation of protection, ensuring victory over the attacks and pressures of Satan's kingdom.

A PRAYER TO PUT ON THE HELMET

Loving Heavenly Father, I take by faith the helmet of salvation. I recognize that my salvation is the Person of Your Son, the Lord Jesus Christ. I cover my mind with Him. I desire that He put His mind within me. Let my thoughts be His thoughts. I open my mind fully and only to the control of the Lord Jesus Christ. Replace my own selfish and sinful thoughts with His. I reject every projected thought of Satan and his demons and request instead the mind of the Lord Jesus Christ. Grant to me the wisdom to discern thoughts that are from the world, my old sin nature, and Satan's kingdom.

I praise You that I may know the mind of Christ as I hide Your Word within my heart and mind. Open my heart to love Your Word. Grant to me the facility and capacity to memorize large portions of it. May Your Word be ever over my mind like a helmet of strength, which Satan's projected thoughts cannot penetrate.

Forgive me for my neglect, my failure to aggressively take the salvation always available to me. Help me to fulfill the discipline of daily duty to appropriate Your salvation. These things I lay before You in the precious name of my Savior, the Lord Jesus Christ. Amen.

10

THE SWORD
OF THE SPIRIT

*Take . . . the sword of the Spirit, which is the word
of God. (Ephesians 6:17b)*

When the apostle Peter made his great confession to the
Lord Jesus, "You are the Messiah, the Son of the living
God," Jesus gave a challenging response: "And I tell you that you
are Peter, and on this rock I will build my church, and the gates
of Hades will not overcome it. I will give you the keys of the
kingdom of heaven; whatever you bind on earth will be bound
in heaven, and whatever you loose on earth will be loosed in
heaven" (Matthew 16:16, 18–19).

That is a promise setting forth the opportunity every believer
has to aggressively overcome Satan's kingdom. Ours needs to be
much more than merely a defensive battle. We have opportunity
to be aggressive and actually to invade Satan's kingdom. Hell, or
Hades in this text, refers to the unseen world of fallen beings.
For a number of years I saw that passage only as a promise from
our Lord to protect His church from the attacks of Satan. That
thought is certainly there, but the promise goes far beyond that.
The Greek word *katischuo*, translated "overcome" or "prevail," literally means "shall not prove stronger." The primary purpose of
Satan's gates is to protect what he claims as his own. He wants to

hold onto what belongs to him and build such strong gates that we cannot take away any of what he claims. Our Lord is saying that His church will be able to go right through those gates and take from Satan what he would like to keep as his own.

BINDING AND ROBBING OUR ENEMY

When the Pharisees accused Jesus of driving out demons by the power of "Beelzebub, the prince of demons," both Matthew and Mark record that our Lord knew their thoughts and showed that Satan's kingdom could not stand if it were as divided as they said (Matthew 12:22–29; Mark 3:22–27). He then made a most dramatic statement that applies to our victory over Satan: "How can anyone enter a strong man's house and carry off his possessions unless he first ties up the strong man? Then he can plunder his house" (Matthew 12:29). As believers, united with Christ in His authority, we are able to so war against Satan that we can bind him, tie him up, and rob or take away what he wants to claim as his own.

Our stance is not to be one of merely protecting ourselves, as important as that is. We are to see ourselves as invincible soldiers of Christ who can advance against this "strong man," Satan, invade his domain, and take away from him those people and spiritual fortifications he claims. The other parts of the armor in Ephesians 6 are mainly protective and defensive, but now we come to see that our spiritual sight must extend beyond the defensive stance. The "sword of the Spirit" is an offensive weapon as well as a means of defense. The analogy of a human army may serve to help us see this truth.

Suppose a modern day army were to specialize only in defense. The troops would have the strongest, most bullet-resistant helmets available. Each soldier would be equipped with vests that could not be penetrated by modern rifles. They would have tanks with the thickest armor, jet fighters with the fastest speed and maneuverability, and every other protective weaponry imaginable. There is only one problem. This defensive army has no bullets, guns, rockets, bombs, or artillery. What would happen to such an army against an aggressive enemy? That enemy, though not as well-equipped defensively, will just keep pounding away at the defense, and eventually the pounding will get through. The old adage "The best defense is a good offense" has application in spiritual warfare too. "For though we live in the world, we do not wage war as the world does. The weapons we fight with are not the weapons of the world. On the contrary, they have divine power to demolish strongholds" (2 Corinthians 10:3–4). Though Satan presses a relentless battle against every believer, the believer who sees that he is responsible to carry the battle to the enemy is the one who wins.

A Christian man experiencing a severe battle with Satan and his demon kingdom sought my counsel. The powers of darkness were suggesting to him such thoughts as "Curse God," "Tear up the Bible," "Set the church on fire," and others of an even more vulgar nature. After carefully teaching and encouraging him in his warfare, I instructed him to react aggressively against the thoughts that seemed demonic in origin. I urged him when such thoughts came to say something like this: "I reject these thoughts to curse God and choose instead to honor the Lord. In the name of the Lord Jesus Christ, I bind the power of darkness that projects these thoughts into my mind, and I command you and all who work with you to leave me and to go where the Lord Jesus Christ sends you."

His response was typical of many people who are under such oppression. He had been intimidated so long by the fierce opposition of Satan that he said to me, "Can I do that? I'm afraid to do that. I'm just a man, and Satan is so powerful."

Satan would like to keep us thinking such error. He always wants to keep us from going on the offensive.

OUR OFFENSIVE WEAPONS

We have essentially two offensive weapons to use against Satan. They are the Word of God and prayer. In the days of the early church, the apostles were leading the fight, carrying the battle to the enemy, and invading his gates. You cannot do that without a proper emphasis upon the offensive weapons. Acts 6 describes what happened when the need arose for someone to take over the daily distribution of food to widows. The church chose the first representatives for church ministry so that the apostles might "turn this responsibility over to them and . . . give [their] attention to prayer and the ministry of the word" (Acts 6:3–4). Progress in the Lord's work requires an aggressive use of prayer and our sword, God's Word.

The sword is last on the list of the parts of armor. Why would that be?

One reason is we are not ready to use our aggressive weapon against Satan's kingdom until all the other parts of the armor are in place. None of us is ready to march into battle without our armor. The sword is listed last as a warning against presumptuous, foolhardy warfare. In our bold view of invincible warfare we must never forget who our enemy is. He is the most powerful of all created beings. He was a formidable foe to even Michael the archangel. "But even the archangel Michael, when he was disputing with the devil about the body of Moses, did not himself dare to condemn him for slander, but said, 'The Lord rebuke you!'" (Jude 9). That verse comes in a section warning those who "reject authority and heap abuse on celestial beings" (Jude 8).

Though we have authority as believers to be bold and fearless in our battle with Satan, we do not have the right to be flippant or presumptuous. The basis of our victory is that we are united with Christ, who has defeated Satan. Even the Lord Jesus in His encounters with Satan resisted the devil with dignity and proper respect for Satan's created role (Matthew 4:1–11). As mentioned in chapter 3, Acts 19:13–20 provides an illustration of some people who went into battle with the powers of darkness in a presumptuous and foolhardy way. The seven sons of Sceva, a Jewish chief priest, saw Paul invoking the name of the Lord Jesus Christ over people who were demonized, thus setting them free from their bondage. They believed that they too might use the name of the Lord Jesus to deliver people so afflicted and tried to use the formula "In the name of the Jesus whom Paul preaches, I command you to come out." The response from the demon was clear: "Jesus I know, and Paul I know about, but who are you?" At that point, the man controlled by the wicked spirit "jumped on them and overpowered them all. He gave them such a beating that they ran out of the house naked and bleeding" (Acts 19:13–16).

The message of this incident ought to be clear. One cannot trifle with Satan's kingdom. Although the men were probably not yet believers in the Lord Jesus Christ, the warning has application to true believers today. A careless, unprepared advance against Satan's kingdom that lacks full awareness of our union with Christ, the ministry of the Holy Spirit, and the provision of our armor may prove disastrous.

Missionaries have gotten into trouble by careless approach to the battle. I have known of several who have experienced severe problems when they treated such things lightly. One missionary friend had dismissed fetishes and wooden idols dedicated to Satan worship as having little significance. Upon the conversion of a witch doctor, he asked to have the witch doctor's fetishes and idols to keep and show as missionary artifacts. The consequences almost proved permanently disastrous. Afflictions and severe problems came upon him and his family. The oppression was devastating. It appeared for a time that he would not be able to continue his missionary service. Finally the items were burned, and he sought the Lord's forgiveness for his careless attitude about the realness of Satan's power.

THE POWER OF GOD'S WORD

The sword of the Spirit is the *Word of God*. In keeping with John 1:1, the Lord Jesus is often spoken of as "the living Word" just as the Bible is the written Word. We have to be careful, however, not to deify the written Word to the point that we worship it. We must worship not the Bible, but the God of the Bible. Yet, because it is the very Word of God and will never pass away, the Bible carries many of the attributes of God Himself.

It is the eternal Word just as God Himself is eternal. As God is omnipotent, so does His Word have all power to defeat Satan and to accomplish God's will. As God is immutable, so the Word of God will never change. As our Lord is omnipresent, so His Word is always there and ready to be used in every situation. As God is holy, so His Word is holy. The writer to the Hebrews says "The word of God is alive and active. Sharper than any double-edged sword, it penetrates even to dividing soul and spirit, joints and marrow; it judges the thoughts and attitudes of the heart" (Hebrews 4:12).

THE INNER WORKING OF THE WORD

The sword of the Word has the power to penetrate one's life. It is meant to perform corrective surgery within the soul, spirit, thoughts, and attitudes of the believer. That is perhaps the secret of its power against Satan. As the believer uses it, the Word can penetrate, cleanse, and change the believer's life and in so doing, cut away Satan's grip upon that life.

Nothing is quite as important in spiritual warfare as getting the Word of God into the mind and heart of the believer. That one thing will accomplish more in setting a person free from Satan's oppression and affliction than any other method I know.

A Christian brother who had come under severe oppression from the enemy was for years unable to work or to attend church. He withdrew from life and duty. Fear, depression, and torment seemed to rule his life. Then victory began to come as he started memorizing large portions of God's Word. Daily he meditated on Scripture passages and repeated their meaning. It was amazing to see the change that simple procedure effected in his life. Anyone who is serious about spiritual warfare must memorize the Word and meditate upon it daily, even hourly.

There is no substitute for persistent, steady, consistent application of God's Word against Satan. The Lord Jesus Christ used that approach in His dramatic encounter with Satan in the wilderness, recorded in Luke 4:1–13.

He had fasted for forty days. At the end of that time Jesus was hungry, and food was many miles away. Satan tempted our Lord, saying: "If you are the Son of God, tell this stone to become bread" (Matthew 4:3). In reply, Jesus quoted from Deuteronomy 8:3, "It is written: 'Man shall not live on bread alone' " (Luke 4:4).

Next Satan tried to tempt the Lord Jesus to take a shortcut to the glory of His coming kingdom by worshiping him. Again Christ quoted the Word: "It is written: 'Worship the Lord your God and serve him only' " (Luke 4:8).

The final temptation came at the highest point of the Temple in Jerusalem, where Satan tried to get Jesus to "throw yourself down from here." That time, Satan himself quoted the Scriptures, from Psalm 91:11–12. Once again the Lord Jesus Christ used the weapon of the Word, quoting Deuteronomy 6:16: "It is said: 'Do not put the Lord your God to the test' " (Luke 4:12). At that point, the devil left Jesus "until an opportune time" (Luke 4:13). He was defeated by the Savior's persistent use of the "sword" but was determined to try again.

Servants of Christ will find Satan using the same pattern of attack against them. And Satan will leave only as the Word of God is persistently applied against him.

GUIDELINES
FOR USING THE SWORD

One of the most obvious requirements for using the "sword" is to *know the Word of God.* It was the accepted practice for devout Jewish boys during our Lord's earthly life to memorize the first five books of the Old Testament. For most of us, that would seem an impossible task, yet there are people living today who have committed the entire New Testament to memory. Others know large portions of both Testaments. It seems obvious that the Lord Jesus Christ's ability to quickly quote from the book of Deuteronomy was a key to Satan's defeat.

Scripture memorization is one of the most urgently needed disciplines of the Christian home and the church. If we are not equipping ourselves for battle by memorizing the Word, our best weapon will be just out of our reach when we need it most. Satan is waiting to find "an opportune time" in each of our lives. That opportune time will arise when we have no Bible nearby, and our weapon will be out of reach if we do not have it memorized.

There are many ways to memorize Scripture. Some can memorize large sections of the Word by simply reading them many times. For many years, when visiting hospital patients, I read favorite passages of the Word that spoke of the Lord's comfort. One day, having left my Bible in the car, I discovered to my surprise that I could quote those portions almost perfectly. Others find it helpful to write out verses or paragraphs on cards to carry with them and then work on memorizing them in spare moments. It is helpful to work with another person when memorizing, so you can check on each other. Most people work more effectively under the principle of accountability.

It is equally important that you correctly *understand the Word of God*. One who memorizes the Word must also be one who "correctly handles the word of truth" (2 Timothy 2:15). When Satan quoted the Scriptures to Jesus during His temptation, he misinterpreted them. That is one of Satan's most clever tricks. He wants us to misunderstand and misuse the Word. Some of the most effective human instruments Satan has are people who use the Bible effusively, but incorrectly.

When memorizing the Word of God, it is effective to express in your own words what the text is saying. If you have any doubt about the meaning, use a trustworthy Bible commentary to arrive at a correct understanding.

Satan may use a wrong understanding of a passage of Scripture to paralyze a Christian's effectiveness. One day I had a phone call from a Christian lady who was in severe distress. She was the wife of a prominent physician in a distant city and they were actively committed to a Bible-preaching church. She had got into a great deal of difficulty over two passages of Scripture in the book of Hebrews (6:4–6; 10:26–31). Satan kept tormenting her into believing that she had "fallen away" and that she had lost her salvation and could not be saved again. In trying to help, I asked her if she had ever prayed over those passages, repeatedly read them, and sought to understand what they really said. "Oh, no," was her reply. "They always frighten me too much, and I try not to read them."

Her response was typical of how Satan tries to misuse the Word of God. By tormenting her, the enemy was able to keep her from mastering the Word. I urged her to make an exhaustive study of those passages. Admittedly, they are some of the most difficult texts to understand, and I assured her that she would find good Bible scholars differing in their approach to those texts. Yet, the Word is the truth of God, and God wants us to know it.

We must know the Scripture and insist that the enemy acknowledge our stand. We can do this effectively only as we build our lives upon God's Word, "rooted and grounded" in the truth. We cannot build effective warfare upon anything else. Feelings will not do. Feelings are as changeable as the wind. Our own discipline and dedication will not do. One day we experience emotional highs, and another day emotional lows. Only the Word of God effectively dispatches the enemy.

Satan will not easily back off from you even when you use the Word against him. He will test you and try to get you to doubt the truth of the Word. He will challenge you. It is always important to establish your authority over him because of your union with Christ. The enemy may deny that Christ has authority over him. But if you know the Word and quote the Word, establishing Christ's authority, you can always force him to admit that Christ has authority over all principalities and powers (Ephesians 1:19–22; Philippians 2:9–11).

THE PERSON OF THE SPIRIT

We must not fail to recognize that the power behind "the sword of the Spirit" is a Person, the Holy Spirit. He is the one who makes our sword effective in battle.

Peter's experience in the garden when men came to take Jesus is an example of a believer's swinging the wrong sword (John 18:10). He used the wrong sword and was trusting in the wrong strength to be effective in battle. The only result was that Malchus lost an ear. If our Lord had not been there to heal the ear immediately, not only would Malchus have suffered injury, but the entire company of disciples could have been arrested, perhaps imprisoned, or even crucified with Jesus. Our Lord often has to rescue us when we go about swinging the wrong sword in spiritual battle. Later that same man, Peter, swung the sword of the Spirit on the day of Pentecost. Instead of injuring one man's ear, he captured and spiritually healed three thousand "ears." Three thousand people responded to the Word of salvation and were baptized as believers.

We cannot effectively use the Word of God in warfare unless the Holy Spirit is controlling us. "But the fruit of the Spirit is love, joy, peace, patience, kindness, goodness, faithfulness, gentleness, self-control; against such things there is no law" (Galatians 5:22–23 ESV). We cannot fight spiritual battles in a fleshly way.

In the early years of my ministry, one member of the church I pastored was very difficult to work with. She had a sharp tongue, a quick temper, and was somewhat overbearing. She had offended many people over the years. It would have been fairly easy to have asked her to leave the church, as some of the deacons wanted to do. After a couple of sharp encounters with her myself, I felt that might not be a bad idea. I went so far as to pray about it. Afterward, I remember thinking, *If I do that, God will give me two more just like her.* God had put her there for me to love, to nurture, to train, to feed, and to lead, not to kick out. How often we get into trouble when we resort to a method other than that "of the Spirit." Satan moves in on such situations even when we feel we are right and the other person is wrong. He indeed may be very wrong, but we can never do good things in a fleshly way.

We must also remember not to resist the Holy Spirit in one area of life while trying to use the "sword of the Spirit" in another. Several years ago, a woman who was under severe assault from the powers of darkness came to me for counseling. I used all the methods of warfare I knew but was still not very successful. After several weeks of counseling, I could see no improvement. She was memorizing the Word, practicing aggressive resistance of the enemy, praying doctrinally-oriented prayers, but still seemed to be losing the battle. I finally concluded something was seriously wrong.

In kindness, I asked her if she was resisting the Holy Spirit in some area. She hung her head and finally told me she had a smoking problem. She did not smoke heavily, but she was aware that it was a habit she would not submit to the Holy Spirit. We dealt with that, and immediate improvement began. The intensity of the battle subsided, and the last I knew, she was walking tall in victory.

It is the Holy Spirit who applies the power of the "sword" against our foe. If we are grieving or quenching His work in our lives in any area, Satan will be quick to take advantage of that opening.

All spiritual victory is essentially bound to the Word of God. Satan retreats as the Word of God, the sword of the Spirit, is used against him.

A PRAYER TO TAKE UP THE SWORD

In the name of the Lord Jesus Christ, I lay hold of the sword of the Spirit, the Word of God. I embrace its inerrant message of truth and power. I humbly ask the Holy Spirit to guide me into true understanding of the message of the Word. Grant to me the discipline and dedication to memorize the Word and to saturate my mind with its truth and power.

In the name of the Lord Jesus Christ and by the ministry of the Holy Spirit, grant to me the wisdom to always apply the Word against the enemy. May I use the Word to defeat Satan and to advance the cause of Christ into that very realm Satan claims. Amen.

PART IV

THE WEAPON
OF PRAYER

And pray in the Spirit on all occasions
with all kinds of prayers and requests.
With this in mind, be alert and always keep on praying for
all the Lord's people.

EPHESIANS 6:18

11

THE ALLNESS
OF PRAYER

My mother was born on a farm in Iowa shortly after her parents emigrated from Scotland. She knew what it was like to work hard and to stretch meager funds to meet the many demands of life. Poverty did not dull her spirit, though, and eventually better times came into her life. She married a prosperous young farmer. He built a spacious new home with many of the modern conveniences other farm homes did not have. They were blessed with three healthy sons, keeping her busy but happy and fulfilled. The farm did well, and the future seemed bright with promise. She came to know Christ as her Savior, and after her conversion, God's blessings seemed to have no end. All seemed right with her world.

Then, like a sudden storm unleashing its fury, heartbreaking disappointment fell upon her. One heartache mounted on top of another. During the Great Depression, my father lost one farm and was in danger of losing our home. In the midst of financial trial, Mother gave birth to her first and only daughter, a beautiful baby with a serious birth defect—who lived only three days. The beloved church where Mother had found Christ closed its doors, and the building was sold. Then, illness added its burden. Her youngest son went from one siege of double pneumonia into another, and as the doctor left the house one day, he said, "He cannot live through the night."

Heartbroken, frightened, and desperate, her overwhelming needs closed in upon her. What could she do? Who could help? She had no pastor to call. Even family and Christian friends were not near.

Overwhelmed, she fled to her room and fell onto her knees. My father joined her in prayer for a time, but sleep eventually overtook him. She could not sleep, however. She kept praying, shut in with God for most of the night. In the midst of prayer, a method of treating her son's pneumonia came to her mind. She felt the idea for treatment to be a leading from the Lord. She applied it, and her son's life was saved. Courage and faith were born anew in her heart. Perhaps of more importance, in that moment of need she learned of a greatness in prayer that continued to characterize the rest of her life.

I was that son who was healed of pneumonia. I have many beautiful memories of that noble woman who was my mother, but the crowning memory is the greatness and power of her prayer life. How very fortunate is that person who, when surrounded by overwhelming trials and burdens, learns to pray. It took me many years to learn that myself.

Ephesians 6:18 tells us to "pray in the Spirit on all occasions with all kinds of prayers and requests. With this in mind, be alert and always keep on praying for all the Lord's people."

That verse helps to convey the all-importance of prayer for being invincible to do the will of God. Four times the concept of "allness" is presented. Prayer is not simply an indispensable, additional part of the believer's armor, but rather is of equal importance as the other parts.

We have covered the four keys to victory as set forth in Ephesians 6:10–18:

1. The believer's position and relationship to Christ. "Finally, be strong in the Lord" (Ephesians 6:10a). Our inseparable union with Christ in all His Person and work makes us invincible.
2. The work and ministry of the Holy Spirit. "Be strong . . . in his mighty power" (Ephesians 6:10b). We are able to enjoy and experience "his mighty power" only as the Holy Spirit fills and empowers us (Acts 1:8; Ephesians 3:16).
3. The whole armor of God (Ephesians 6:11–17). As we carefully clothe ourselves, in faith, with that spiritual clothing, we become a formidable opponent to the powers of darkness.
4. The absolute necessity of prayer. The apostle Paul repeatedly calls our attention to the importance of prayer in the book of Ephesians. In 1:15–23, Paul reveals the intensity of his own prayers for the Ephesian believers. Warren Wiersbe points out that in this prayer "he does not ask God to give them what they do not have, but rather prays that God will reveal to them what they already have."[1]

In Ephesians 3:14–21, Paul presents a picture of himself bowing in prayer before the heavenly Father. He prays that the Ephesians might be enabled to do God's will. The burden of his prayer is that those believers might lay hold of the "glorious riches" available in Christ (Ephesians 3:16), which are "immeasurably more than all we ask or imagine" (Ephesians 3:20). Through those riches we are able to be energized by the power of the Spirit and to enjoy "the fullness

> Prayer is not simply an indispensable, additional part of the believer's armor, but rather is of equal importance as the other parts.

of God" (Ephesians 3:19). Prayer is the key to *enlightenment* and *enablement* in enjoying the "glorious riches" of God.

THE PREEMINENCE OF PRAYER

In Ephesians 6:18, Paul admonishes us to pray "on all occasions," or "in all seasons." That means to pray when you feel like it and when you don't feel like it. The preeminence of prayer needs to be firmly settled in our minds. There is no place for halfhearted, passive involvement when it comes to warfare praying.

A. T. Pierson wrote,

> Every new Pentecost has had its preparatory period of supplement—of waiting for enduement; and sometimes the time of tarrying has been lengthened from "ten days" to as many weeks, months, or even years; but never has there been an outpouring of the Divine Spirit from God without a previous outpouring of the human spirit toward God. To vindicate this statement would require us to trace the whole history of missions, for the field of such display of divine power covers the ages. Yet every missionary biography, from those of Elliot and Edwards, Brainerd and Carey, down to Livingstone and Burns, Hudson Taylor and John E. Clough, tells the same story: prayer has been the preparation for every new triumph; and so, if greater triumphs and successes lie before us, more fervent and faithful praying must be their forerunner and herald![2]

It is impossible to overemphasize the role of biblical prayer in the victory of believers.

THE PASSION OF PRAYER

We are to pray "with all kinds of prayers and requests." Have you ever considered how many different kinds of prayers there are? There is silent prayer and audible prayer, prayer without ceasing and prayer that terminates, public prayer and private prayer, short prayer and extended prayer, fasting prayer and feasting prayer, prayer with one's actions and prayer with one's words, rejoicing prayer and broken prayer, thanksgiving prayer and petitioning prayer, doctrinal prayer and emotional prayer, resisting-the-enemy prayer and standing-with-the-Lord prayer. There are probably other kinds of prayers we could consider, but the truth is that all kinds of prayers are a part of our warfare.

At times it is important just to praise the Lord in prayer. I recall an occasion when a distraught husband brought his troubled wife to counsel with me. She was under severe affliction from demonic powers. Although she did not know where our house was, the powers of darkness afflicting her did. As they neared our home, she began to scream uncontrollably and tried to jump out of the moving car. With considerable difficulty, the husband was able to steer her through our door and into a private counseling room. There she was like a frightened, caged animal, trying to flee, only to be blocked by her husband. When I could gain no communication with her, the Holy Spirit led me to praise the Lord in prayer and song. I began to pray a doctrinal prayer of praise, enumerating the wondrous attributes of God and describing what it means to abide in Christ. At first there seemed to be a violent reaction from the powers of darkness afflicting her. But as the praise continued, Satan's power was broken, and she became calm as the "peace of God" settled upon her.

Resisting the enemy in prayer is something we do not do as often as we should. "For though we live in the world, we do not wage war as the world does. The weapons we fight with are not the weapons of the world. On the contrary, they have divine power to demolish strongholds" (2 Corinthians 10:3–4). What a challenge that verse is to us—that we would see our "divine power" to resist the strategies of Satan. Joshua and the people of Israel achieved the same kind of victory against Jericho. The walls of the enemy were so thick and strong that there seemed to be no way Israel could take that mighty city. Yet by prayer and obedience to the Word of the Lord, the walls fell. They didn't even throw a stone. That is the way it is in spiritual warfare. Impossible fortifications crumble to dust before the believers who use the divine power of their weapons to pull down strongholds. Like Israel, we can then walk through the gates and plunder the enemy's land.

Do you schedule an hour or two with God several times each week? Martin Luther prayed the first two hours of his day—every day. Spurgeon had shut-away times when it was said not even a visit from the King of England would cause him to interrupt his prayer.

The Greek word translated "supplication" literally means "the character of necessity or compulsion in prayer." To bind yourself to the Lord with such a tie of petition is to ensure the answer. Every prayer has an answer, even if it is "No" or "Wait."

THE PARACLETE OF PRAYER

We are to pray "in the Spirit." Some would interpret this to mean that we must pray in "tongues." The Bible indicates otherwise. Paul's prayers in Ephesians 1 and 3 were certainly "in the Spirit" and were not uttered in "tongues."

I give a word of warning to those who seek to "pray in tongues." To those who have shared their experiences with me, I ask, "Have you tested the spirit authoring your 'tongue'?" The Holy Spirit Himself tells us to do that in 1 John 4:1–4. While a person prays in a "tongue," his own mind is largely in a neutral state. I suggest that he command the spirit authoring the tongue to answer clearly in his mind, "Has Jesus Christ come in the flesh? Is Jesus Christ Lord? Do you honor the blood of Jesus Christ?" Insist upon a clear and precise answer. The Holy Spirit will always answer with rejoicing "Yes!" Another spirit will be evasive or even on some occasions give a blatant "No." It is important to avoid being deceived by a "lying spirit," lest Satan gain an advantage against us.

Praying in the Spirit means praying in harmony with the Spirit or under the control of the Spirit. Several practical steps will ensure that we are praying in the Spirit. First, we must ask the Holy Spirit to control our praying and to guide us to pray in harmony with His will. That is one of the Holy Spirit's ministries according to Romans 8:26–27: "In the same way, the Spirit helps us in our weakness. We do not know what we ought to pray for, but the Spirit himself intercedes for us through wordless groans. And he who searches our hearts knows the mind of the Spirit, because the Spirit intercedes for God's people in accordance with the will of God."

We also need to deliberately reject all fleshly praying. James warns, "When you ask, you do not receive, because you ask with wrong motives, that you may spend what you get on your pleasures" (James 4:3). It is good to say as one begins to pray, "In the name of the Lord Jesus Christ I reject the involvement of my old sin nature in my prayer. I count myself dead with Christ to my sin nature and its control, and I ask the Holy Spirit to sovereignly oversee the words of my prayer."

A third suggestion is to pray in harmony with the truth of the Word. The Word of God is Holy Spirit breathed (2 Timothy 3:16–17).

When we pray God's Word back to Him, we can be sure that we pray in the Spirit. Memorizing prayers from the Psalms or other great prayers of the Bible is a way to be sure of praying in the Spirit. One can certainly pray in the Spirit if he prays a prayer like Paul's prayer for the Ephesian believers in Ephesians 3:14–21. It is good to master such passages in order to know how to pray for yourself and your church. Matthew 6:9–13, the "Lord's

Prayer," can serve as a good guideline for praying in the Spirit.

Probably all of us have experienced times of prayer when the words flowed easily and the heart was warm toward God. Sometimes we interpret those prayers as being in the Spirit, whereas difficult times are regarded as not being so. Yet, many of the prayers recorded in the Psalms begin with the lament that God seems far off and silent (see Psalms 28, 55, 102).

For a number of years, I sensed barriers and walls during shut-away times of in-depth prayer. How glad I was to realize that such times of prayer can also be in the Spirit. The deep emotion of such times often teaches us more and expresses our needs more effectively than times of greater liberty do. Doctrinal praying—praying the truth of God's Word back to Him—will aid in breaking through the times when barriers seem to hide God's face from us.

THE PROTECTION OF PRAYER

"With this in mind, be alert." This phrase has a military ring to it. It conveys the picture of a sentry on duty, guarding something that needs protection. In spiritual warfare, believers must stand guard through prayer, watching over themselves, their families, their church, and the work to which the Lord has called them.

In the military, someone on sentry duty stands guard to prevent surprise attack from unseen enemies. When she was still living, my wife's mother always included in her prayers the words "Protect us from dangers and enemies, seen and unseen." She was "being alert," and every time I heard her pray that way, I was always impressed. Who can know what terrible calamities are avoided by alert praying.

The Lord Jesus employed that kind of warfare praying. To Peter the Lord Jesus said, "Simon, Simon, Satan has asked to sift all of you as wheat. But I have prayed for you, Simon, that your faith may not fail. And when you have turned back, strengthen your brothers" (Luke 22:31–32). Christ was being alert for Peter and the other apostles. The same kind of "sentry duty" prayer is evidenced in His great high priestly prayer of John 17.

I learned of a missionary who returned home from the field discouraged and broken-hearted, when two of her older children attending school in this country were showing signs of serious rebellion against all that they had been taught and professed to believe. Having always prayed for her children, she was in a quandary about what to do. Someone gave her a copy of *The Adversary*, and she took up the challenge of warfare praying with fervency. She later called me and shared that prayer had dramatically turned around the lives of her children. She returned to the field with a new awareness of her responsibility to be alert for her family.

Satan would like nothing better than to harm us. He would afflict us with illness, misfortune, or misery if he had but one opportunity. When employing protective warfare praying, we can watch for ways that the Lord protects us.

One Saturday morning, my wife and I were driving home in separate cars from an early morning prayer meeting at our church. While I watched in my rearview mirror to see that my wife was following me, she arrived at an intersection just as a careless driver, traveling much too fast, sped through, barely missing her car. For a moment, it seemed certain that an accident would occur. Yet, as I viewed the whole thing in my rearview mirror, restful assurance flooded my soul. That very morning I had carefully watched over my entire family in warfare prayer. Guardian angels and a sovereign, protecting Shepherd were on duty in answer to my prayer. Just another near miss? No, I'm certain it wasn't.

THE PERSEVERANCE
OF PRAYER

There is no more important word than *persistence* in warfare praying. We need to claim daily our union with Christ, appropriate the Holy Spirit's work, put on each part of the armor, and employ persistent prayer. Many times a day we may be called upon to use those elements in our efforts to win the battle. We must be persistent. We must not let down if things are going well and suppose such faithful warfare is not necessary.

A man shared with me his problem with lust and pornography. We considered carefully the steps to overcoming the lusts of the flesh. First, we talked about the need to be honest and admit to oneself and to God that the old sin nature was at work. Then we went over the need to reckon oneself dead with Christ to the rule and reign of that sin (Romans 6:11). We can by faith affirm that to be true, because it is true. We are responsible to "not let sin reign in [our] mortal bod[ies]" (Romans 6:12). The only way we can do that is to recognize that we have been crucified with Christ (Galatians 2:20). Third, we discussed the need to ask the Holy Spirit to replace our fleshly, sinful desires with desires marked by the fruit of the Spirit: "love, joy, peace, patience, kindness, goodness, faithfulness, gentleness, self-control" (Galatians 5:22–23 ESV).

We went over those three steps until he could repeat them back to me, and he promised to use them each time he came under temptation.

A few weeks later he came into my study, slumped in a chair, and groaned about being defeated by the lusts of the flesh. I listened attentively and sympathetically for a time, but then I asked him, "What are the biblical steps to overcoming your sin nature?" He was stumped. He remembered we had talked about that previously, but he couldn't recall what the three steps were.

Once again we went over them. I showed him carefully that each of those three steps is set forth as God's way to victory over the flesh. I kept encouraging him until he could repeat them back to me. I then told him that until he put those steps into consistent practice, I could do no more for him. Even God could do nothing more for him until he began to use what had already been provided.

We must also be *insistent*. It would be much easier if our enemy were willing to admit that we have full authority over him because we are united with Christ in all of His victory. Yet, he is not that kind of enemy. He but grudgingly admits such victory. Most of us have observed a disobedient child reluctantly giving in to the authority of his parent. He doesn't give an inch until he absolutely has to. Satan and his demons are like that. This is why in warfare our prayer needs to be insistent in our persistence. There are times in all of our lives when everything seems to be failing and the enemy seems to be winning at every turn. That is the very time we need to be most insistent that he just can't win.

In Acts 16, Paul and Silas successfully cast out a demon from a young fortune-teller. Those who made money from her fortune-telling had Paul and Silas arrested, roughly handled, and finally put in a dungeon, locked up in stocks. That pictures Satan's refusal to admit he is defeated. Instead of feeling sorry for themselves and complaining about how the devil was beating them, they prayed and sang songs of victory. The other prisoners all heard them at midnight. In faith and practice, despite outward evidence to the contrary, they just kept insisting on their victory. Suddenly the prison shook, their stocks fell off, the doors opened, and they were free. The victory went on to such a dimension that the jailer and his family were saved, and the town authorities who had treated them so badly had to apologize (see Acts 16). Truth must win. Persistence faces all tests and keeps on insisting that evil must yield to truth.

THE PANORAMA OF PRAYER

Warfare prayer is to be "for all the Lord's people" (Ephesians 6:18). Does that take your breath away as it did mine the first time I saw it? What a vast spectrum of responsibility we have in warfare praying. It can be viewed as an ever-widening series of circles extending outward. Your first responsibility is for yourself. Each believer has the care of his own life and ministry to oversee. The next step out is your family. No one will watch over your family in prayer as you will. The circles then extend to your church, your denomination, your missionaries, and the entire Body of Christ around the world. Christ commanded the disciples to witness to Jerusalem, Judea, Samaria, and the uttermost parts of the earth. "For all the Lord's people" prayer reaches out that far, too. It has a panorama of responsibility that embraces the whole world.

Since being on a preaching mission to Britain in 1964, I have felt a special prayer responsibility for that nation. Many times as I have wrestled in prayer for the believers there and for revival in Britain, the Holy Spirit has broken my heart to tears for that nation. Others have felt the same concern for China.

THE PROJECTION OF PRAYER

In Ephesians 6:18, we see that prayer should be projected to "all the Lord's people." In verses 19 and 20 we see that warfare prayer can specifically be projected toward the effectiveness of our ministry.

Paul asks the Ephesians: "Pray also for me, that whenever I speak, words may be given" (Ephesians 6:19). He is saying that the warfare prayer of the Ephesian believers can enable him to have greater ability to communicate the gospel. Every preacher knows the truth of those words. All of us have had the experience of studying hard and preparing diligently, only to try to deliver the message and find the words will not come. My wife has developed a capacity to know when I am facing such a trial. I have often seen her bow her head in prayer to ask that "words may be given." And often the barriers have been broken on such occasions.

That kind of prayer also effects boldness in proclaiming the gospel. Paul says their prayers for him will enable him to "fearlessly make known the mystery of the gospel" (Ephesians 6:19). We not only need to pray for fearless preaching, but we need to pray for open ears.

Prayer directly affects how people hear the Word. That is why prayer support for revival crusades can help bring many souls to Christ. It helps to remove the spiritual blindness and deafness that Satan wants to perpetuate (see 2 Corinthians 4:4). There is no force in the hands of humans as effective and far-reaching as prayer. From the journal of David Brainerd comes this insight:

> In the afternoon God was with me of a truth. Oh, it was blessed company indeed! God enabled me so to agonize in prayer that I was quite wet with sweat, though in the shade and cool wind. My soul was drawn out very much for the world; I grasped for multitudes of souls. I think I had more enlargement for sinners than for the children of God, though I felt as if I could spend my life in cries for both. I had great joy in communion with my dear Saviour. I think I never in my life felt such an entire weanedness from this world, and so much resigned to God in everything. Oh, that I may always live to and upon my blessed God! Amen.[3]

Those are the words of a man who knew something of the allness of prayer. A person of God can literally change the world through prayer without leaving the confines of their own home. The invincible power of prayer knows no bounds.

Notes

1. Warren Wiersbe, *Be Rich* (Wheaton: Scripture Press, 1976), 30.
2. Charles Cook, ed., *Daily Meditations for Prayer* (Westchester: Good News Publishers, n.d.), 27.
3. Jonathan Edwards, *Life and Journal of the Rev. David Brainerd, Missionary to the Indians* (Edinburgh: H. S. Baynes, 1826), 25.

12

INVINCIBLE PRAYER IN ACTION

When I began preparation for the ministry at Moody Bible Institute in Chicago, one of my first assignments was Sunday visitation at the huge Cook County Hospital. A group of us would station ourselves at the hospital entrances, ready to hand out gospel tracts as visitors arrived. I disliked that part of the assignment. People in a hurry to visit loved ones seemed in no mood to be stopped and handed a tract. Some would refuse them; others would crumple them and throw them away. The withering looks of contempt and muttered oaths of disgust I received soon reduced a meek boy from the country into a hiding missionary. I would find a convenient pillar and hide behind it, remaining as much out of the line of traffic as I could. I sincerely hoped no one would come my way, stirring my conscience to hand out a tract.

One Sunday, I was in my favorite hiding place, eagerly waiting for the time I could go to the wards and visit patients. I looked across the lobby and saw a black man handing out tracts. His face was radiant. It seemed to shine with an inner light. His voice was quiet, but its resonant tone reached me across the lobby.

"God bless you, brother. Here's something that will cheer your day." "Jesus loves you, my friend." "Isn't it wonderful to know there is a hope beyond our troubles?" As he handed out the tracts and spoke words of kindness, something amazing happened. People stopped. They took the tracts. Some walked a few steps, stopped, and began to read. Others took the tracts and with what seemed like deliberate reverence, put them into a pocket or purse. I felt sure they intended to read the message later. Even those who refused tracts seemed to walk on with a shamed look.

Others would stop and just look at the man. They seemed captivated by the outflow of his love, arrested by the glow of his goodness.

My interest was aroused. I guess I was somewhat stunned. What accounted for the remarkable contrast between the way people received the tracts from this man and from me? Where did his radiance come from? Why did that quiet voice have such a ring of compelling authority?

Later I learned that radiant man was Chaplain Lilly. He had a fulltime ministry at the hospital, visiting lonely patients and sharing Christ with them. His ministry of love included carrying a shaving kit and barber tools, and he even offered to trim the toenails of patients who lingered many months in the hospital. His words and deeds of love combined brought many to saving faith in Jesus Christ. I longed to know his secret.

It was on the closing Sunday of that assignment that God privileged me to see the answer. Our assignment leader took us on a tour of the hospital. I remember little of that tour except the little "hole in the wall" that was Chaplain Lilly's "office." In one corner was a large overstuffed chair draped with a white sheet. Pointing to the chair, our tour leader said, "That's Chaplain Lilly's throne chair. He never just sits in that chair. Before he goes up to the wards to visit, he often spends hours in prayer for his sick friends and for God's blessing on his ministry."

That's it! I thought. Immediately I knew what accounted for his radiance and the difference in people's response to him. It was prayer. That was one of the greatest lessons God ever taught me. It still lingers in my soul like a special fragrance of grace. One thing will always mark a person who has both power with people and power with God. It will be greatness in prayer. Each significant movement toward God in the spiritual affairs of men and women will be preceded and accompanied by greatness of prayer. "The effective prayer of a righteous man can accomplish much" (James 5:16 NASB).

MOVING GOD TO ACTION

Great prayers get answers. Sometimes all it takes is one person to put God's plan in motion. Armin Gesswein relates the history of a revival that visited Norway in the early 1930s and lasted until the tragic Nazi invasion of that country. For nearly a decade, the awakening moved in numerous churches. As a result, more than 20,000 souls found Christ as Savior and Lord. It was under the preaching of Frank Mangs, an evangelist from Sweden, that the revival spread rapidly to many churches in Norway. He preached for two years, scarcely daring to leave because of the mighty way the Spirit of God was moving. Even after that initial move, he kept returning to preach, and no building would hold the number of people who wanted to hear the Word of God.

Actually, the work of revival had begun some time before Frank Mangs appeared on the scene, in the Betlehem Church in Oslo. The church's prayer meeting had reached such a low point that Pastor Ludvig Johnson was considering discontinuing it. His faithful wife encouraged him: "Dear, we'll keep the prayer meeting even if you and I are the only ones who go." God honored that faith.

But the real secret went back even farther—to the church sexton, a humble man with faith in the invincible power of prayer. He had been disturbed for some time by the coldness of the church and the obvious worldliness of so many of its members.

The sermons seemed dry and dull. Attendance waned, and enthusiasm for prayer and the things of God was low. The sexton asked God what he could do about it. His heart leaped with excitement as by faith he felt a challenge from the Lord. Early in the mornings before he began his duties, he would make his way up behind the pulpit. There he knelt and pleaded for God to revive his heart, his pastor, and the entire church. Holy tears often anointed the carpet as he bent his face low before God in Spirit-led prayer. So sure was this humble servant of God that his prayers would prevail that shortly after the New Year he took the assistant pastor, Holm-Glad, up to the pulpit of the church when no one else was present. He pointed to the empty seats of the church and said, "There is going to be a revival here this year." Holm-Glad said later that he almost laughed because there seemed to be no sign of anything like that. The caretaker, while not sharing his secret of prayer, reaffirmed his certainty that revival would come that year. Weeks passed, then months, and changes began to appear. The pastor's messages began to ring with a new authority, flowing from a heart warmed to God. The prayer meetings began to grow, and crowds began to attend the services. Finally the outbreak of God's Spirit through the preaching of Frank Mangs touched not only that church but also all of Oslo and large areas of Norway.

A year after the revival had broken out, Betlehem Church had a meeting to celebrate the great work of God with a festive dinner followed by a praise service. After the service, the sexton took Pastor Holm-Glad into the sanctuary. With humble tears he said, "Do you remember how I told you there would be a revival here?"

"How could I forget?" responded Holm-Glad.

"Now I am free to tell you how I knew," said the sexton. "Only God knows how many times He burdened my heart to kneel behind the pulpit in prayer for revival. How often I wept sore before the Lord behind this pulpit. We are celebrating today, and God laid it on my heart to tell you this."

I'm so thankful that God burdened that humble, behind-the-scenes servant of the Lord to share that story. How much richer we are to see the invincible power of prayer through any servant who dares to see their invincible position. Great prayer causes God to visibly intervene in human affairs.

Acts 12 records Peter's arrest and imprisonment by Herod. He was scheduled to be tried and probably executed. "So Peter was kept in prison, but the church was earnestly praying to God for him" (Acts 12:5).

Those prayers brought God into action. An angel left heaven's glory to interfere in the plans of the enemy. The chains that bound Peter fell off, and the light of heaven flooded his cell. As he wrapped his garments about him and followed the angel, the prison sentries could not even see Peter. Locked iron gates seemed to come alive and opened at the bidding of heaven's royalty. Unbound and free, Peter went to the prayer meeting, where astonished prayer servants witnessed the living answer to their petitions. God's dramatic, visible movings in response to great prayer stirred a church and defeated the enemy.

ENTERING INTO THE BURDEN

A study of the book of Nehemiah will reveal a striking illustration of greatness in prayer. Nehemiah was in exile in Persia and was serving as cupbearer to the king. As he heard an eyewitness account of the deplorable state of Jerusalem, the tragedy of that great city with broken walls and burned gates broke his heart. Accounts of his Hebrew brethren being greatly afflicted aroused his empathy and moved his soul. Nehemiah was living as a captive in a foreign land, yet he was much better off than those who had escaped capture and stayed in Jerusalem. It was in that hour that he began to pray. He spent many days in tears, fasting, and praying, mourning over the victories God's enemies were having in Jerusalem. The urgency of the need drove him into a greatness of prayer seldom seen among men.

There is no lack of needs today, but few people seem to take responsibility for them like Nehemiah did. Not all believers seem to have the capacity to see need. But even of those who do, only a few seem to let that need take them to the place of greatness in prayer. Some turn away from prayer at such times with the thought, *What's the use anyway? What can I do about it?* Yet, in times of great need, prompt action in faithful prayer can change the course of events.

Sometimes we are not even prepared to devote time and energy to prayer for our own burdens. A woman called me long distance to seek my counsel about her battle with Satan. She insisted that she needed instant deliverance. "I don't want to practice all of this warfare bit. I want you to command Satan to leave me. I want to be done with this battle immediately like Jesus set the man from Gadara free." I have heard similar statements many times from those battling with Satan's kingdom. People want deliverance at the "push of a button." We are the product of our age. In this day of instant soup and immediate computer printouts, we don't want to wait for an answer or carry a burden—even the burden of the Lord.

There is nothing wrong with having a burden so great we must express ourselves in tears, fasting, and extended prayer. Such a burden can be a vital part of living out God's plan. When you experience such a burden, it is good to remember the wise words of an elderly but unlearned man of God. When asked what Scripture passage was his favorite, he admitted that he liked best the words "and it came to pass"—a reoccurring phrase in Scripture. Asked why those words were his favorite, he replied, "Well, it's this way. Whenever I read those blessed words 'and it came to pass', I know that my burdens and troubles ain't come to stay; they's come to pass."

It's obvious that emotionally we could not always carry a burden as heavy as Nehemiah's. God knows that and will see us through to victory in ample time to accomplish His plan. Great needs are meant to bring Christians to their knees in great prayer and ultimately to bring spiritual advancement.

EXPECTING THE VICTORY

One night after midnight, our doorbell rang. I put on my robe and hurried to answer it. Peering through the window in the door, I could see a man I knew who was standing in the cold in his bare feet and dressed only in his pajamas. As I opened the door, he rushed into my arms, pleading for me to help him. I ushered him into a room where we could talk and learned that he felt under attack from the powers of darkness. As a professing Christian, he had been going through some severe trials. On that night, he had awakened with the terrifying sense that some evil powers were trying to take over his being and even kill him.

I began to pray for him, and as I prayed he was seized by some convulsive force that seemed literally to throw him upon the floor. I continued to pray, quoting the Word of God and focusing the victory of Christ upon the man, sometimes commanding any powers of darkness tormenting him to leave him and go where Jesus Christ would send them.

As I continued praying that way, he began to gesture threateningly at me. He was large enough and strong enough to have doubtlessly overpowered me, had he been able to proceed with his threats. I continued to address the promises of the Word against the forces of Satan. As he came toward me, I quoted 1 John 5:18, "He that is begotten of God keepeth himself, and that wicked one toucheth him not" (KJV), and 1 John 3:8, "The Son of

God was manifested, that he might destroy the works of the devil" (KJV). Several times he seemed almost violently thrown back from me. Finally, the war was won. He was calm and able to pray himself and thank the Lord for the victory. He later told me that he seemed controlled by a violent power that strongly wanted to hurt me. Yet each time I addressed the Word of God against the power of darkness seeking to control him, it was as though that violent force was hurled away from me by some invincible power. The Word of God is invincible when rightly understood and applied.

Invincible prayer is centered in great expectancy. Nehemiah expected God to so touch the heart of a pagan king that he would be favorable to rebuilding a walled city that had been destroyed by war. He expected God to incline the king's heart to put him, a cupbearer, in charge of a great expedition to return to Jerusalem to rebuild the walls. Nehemiah expected the Jews in Jerusalem to respond and help him. He expected that the enemies who would oppose the task would be defeated. He expected a government to be reestablished in Jerusalem and the economy to be rebuilt. In short, he expected God to accomplish His will for His people.

And Nehemiah accomplished all that he expected and more. God kept enlarging his expectancy as he moved from victory to victory. The walls were rebuilt. Enemies were defeated. The gates were hung, and city government and worship were reestablished. Confident expectancy is an essential part of the invincible, victorious walk. As His children, we can expect God to accomplish through every one of us His will and purpose for our lives.

A PRAYER FOR TAKING AN INVINCIBLE STANCE

Gracious Heavenly Father, I choose to see myself as You see me in the Person of Your Son, the Lord Jesus Christ. I choose to see myself as invincibly strong and able to do all that is in Your will for me to do. I reject Satan's accusations that I am hopelessly weak and defeated. I accept my present great need as a call to renewed vision of the victory of my Lord. Help me to focus my attention upon the awesome majesty, power, and sovereign greatness of my heavenly Father, who can do anything but fail. Help me to see that in my union with Christ I am more than a conqueror. Let the burden of my trials become an expression of the burden of the Lord. Let that burden be expressed in tears of concern, times of fasting and prayer. I choose not to shrink back from the burden You wish me to carry.

I recognize, Lord, that it is chiefly my own sin and failure that has brought me to this severe trial. I am deeply sorry for my sins. [Mention them by name.] Cleanse me in my Savior's blood. I take back from Satan all ground I have given him by my sins and transgressions. On the authority of the cross I reclaim all of that ground for the Lord Jesus Christ.

Precious Lord Jesus Christ, You have promised never to leave me nor forsake me. I know that is true, and I boldly say, "The Lord is my helper, I will not fear." Steadfast in the faith, I resist the devil and his kingdom. I command Satan and his demons to leave me and to go where the Lord Jesus Christ sends them.

Heavenly Father, I accept and choose to enjoy everything inscribed upon the scroll of Your will for me. Thank You that I can do all things through Christ who is my strength. I will do Your will by accepting my responsibility to be strong. I will do through Your strength the things I know to be Your will. [Tell Him what they are.]

Thank You, loving heavenly Father, that through my Lord Jesus Christ You have heard my prayer—and You will make me to walk as one so strong in the Lord that even Satan's most powerful strategies are already defeated. In the name of the Lord Jesus Christ and for Your glory I pray. Amen.

EPILOGUE

NOTHING BUT A WINNER

To him who is able to keep you from stumbling and to present you before his glorious presence without fault and with great joy—to the only God our Savior be glory, majesty, power and authority, through Jesus Christ our Lord, before all ages, now and forevermore! Amen. (Jude 24–25)

May God himself, the God of peace, sanctify you through and through. May your whole spirit, soul and body be kept blameless at the coming of our Lord Jesus Christ. The one who calls you is faithful, and he will do it. (1 Thessalonians 5:23–24)

Now may the God of peace, who through the blood of the eternal covenant brought back from the dead our Lord Jesus, that great Shepherd of the sheep, equip you with everything good for doing his will, and may he work in us what is pleasing to him, through Jesus Christ, to whom be glory for ever and ever. Amen. (Hebrews 13:20–21)

Now to him who is able to do immeasurably more than all we ask or imagine, according to his power that is at work within us, to him be glory in the church and in Christ Jesus throughout all generations, for ever and ever! Amen. (Ephesians 3:20–21)

Each of those passages is what the church has come to call a benediction, a pronouncement of blessing. Benedictions usually contain summations of great truth designed to comfort, assure, and promote confidence in the hearts of God's people. Those quoted here certainly do that. I would recommend each of them for the reader's memorization and meditation. They assure us that as God's own we are destined to be winners because of the victory Christ has won.

I would like this brief closing to be a kind of benediction to the previous chapters. The message of this book has been an effort to help God's people look beyond the present battle in all its subjective struggle. Through the surety of God's Word, we must fix our attention upon our sure victory: "What then, shall we say in response to this? If God is for us, who can be against us? . . . In all these things we are more than conquerors through him who loved us" (Romans 8:31, 37). Our battle with Satan's dark kingdom is really the Lord's battle. It's a battle that He has already won. It is a victory that He enables us to apply. We have all that we need to resist the enemy in every encounter that he directs against us. The daily aggressive application of our victory assures us of an invincible walk and the fulfillment of God's will.

In *The Adversary,* I relate my daughter Judy's story when she was just a teenager and our family's direct battle with darkness. God used consistent warfare praying and a bold confrontation with the powers of darkness to free her. Forty years have passed since those days of trauma, and she is now a woman deeply in love with her Savior and committed to walking in her freedom in Christ. Judy wrote the preface for the refreshed edition of *The Adversary* and is now working for Moody Publishers and helped me with updating the book you hold in your hands. Though she walks in victory, the years have not been free from attacks from the enemy. Like for every believer, there has been the necessity for spiritual warfare and the application of victory.

I relate Judy's testimony because I want to stress again that the life of victory does not come with a "quick fix" of confrontation and one command for the enemy to leave. That may be necessary in intense times of battle, but that does not end the struggle. Spiritual warfare is a daily walk, a consistent practice, a moment-by-moment readiness to resist every day that we live.

I must also stress that a life of successful spiritual warfare does not guarantee a life without pain and disappointment. Viewed from the short perspective, there will be times when it seems that our enemy has won the day. Such limited sight does not tell the whole story, however. Paul's years of imprisonment at Caesarea and Rome must have seemed to the short-sighted to be a triumph for the enemy. Yet, during those years some of God's greatest victories over darkness were won. Paul's letters to the Ephesians, Philippians, and Colossians were all written from prison. He wrote Ephesians 6:10–18's message of victory, which has been shared through the centuries and around the world. Hold on to the truth that in Christ you are nothing but a winner.

PRAYER
PATTERNS
FOR REVIVAL

PRAYER PATTERNS FOR REVIVAL

Written prayers are not a help to everyone. Some believers prefer to pray from their own minds and hearts. These written prayer patterns for revival are not meant to curtail spontaneous prayer. Written prayers can be helpful when used correctly. There are many written prayers recorded in God's Word that provide patterns and direction for our own praying. Memorizing the prayers in the Psalms or in other portions of the Word provides wonderful help as you pray them back to God out of your own heart.

These prayers are provided to help believers learn to pray doctrinal truth in their intercessions for revival. It is a good practice to write out your own prayers and keep them close so that you can pray them back to God during your shut-away times with Him. Taking time to write down careful expressions of God's Truth greatly honors Him.

I trust that a burden to pray for revival will build in the Body of Christ. I urge each believer to set aside a daily time when a revival prayer focus is expressed.

In God's grace and mercy,

MARK I. BUBECK

These prayers may be reproduced for free distribution when the following credit is attached:

These prayers are available in booklet form
and can be ordered at:

Deeper Walk International, Inc.
info@deeperwalkinternational.org
www.deeperwalkinternational.org

REVIVAL PRAYER PATTERNS

1. FOCUS:
Teach Me to Know You

2. FOCUS:
Repentance and Intercession

3. FOCUS:
Revival Prayer Groups

4. FOCUS:
Protection From the Enemy

5. FOCUS:
Coming Against the Enemy

6. FOCUS:
Unity in the Body

7. FOCUS:
The Word of God

TEN SUGGESTIONS FOR USING PRAYER PATTERNS FOR REVIVAL

1. Pray a different prayer each day so that you cover all seven prayers each week.
2. Use these prayers in family devotional times with each person participating by praying alternate paragraphs.
3. During extended prayer for revival, plan to pray through all seven prayers as part of the time agenda.
4. Distribute the prayers to an entire church body for private and family use.
5. Organize weekly revival prayer groups where some of these prayers are incorporated into the prayer agenda.
6. Carry these prayers in your purse or pocket to use during opportune moments during each day.
7. Keep with you extra Prayer Pattern booklets to share with Christian friends concerned for revival.
8. Plan city-wide revival prayer events where these prayer patterns would inspire believers to revival prayer effort.
9. Mail copies of these prayer patterns to Christian friends around your country and the world.
10. Set aside a day every week or month for fasting and prayer when you plan to address all seven prayers to our Lord.

REVIVAL PRAYER PATTERN 1: TEACH ME TO KNOW YOU

Loving Heavenly Father, I come before You in this time of prayer to open my heart to You about the brokenness and need I see about me. I see great needs in my own heart, in my family, among my fellow believers, and in my culture, community, and world. Teach me to care, and to pray about those needs as Your servant Nehemiah learned to pray. I long to honor You as the "God of heaven, the great and awesome God," whose greatness is sufficient to meet the urgent needs of this day. I long to love and worship You, Heavenly Father, as You are most worthy to be worshiped. I love You, not as perfectly as I one day will, but I do love You and worship You now. Teach me to know You. Even as I worship You this moment, grant me new insights into Your greatness and sufficiency. As I speak to You, please speak to me.

Thank You, Heavenly Father, that You are omnipotent, almighty, and sovereign. I praise You that it was no threat to Your sovereign omnipotence to create Satan and all of the angels who fell, even though You certainly foreknew they would rebel against You. Thank You also, that it was no threat to Your sovereign omnipotence to create man in Your own likeness and image, even though You knew man would fail the test and would sin. I sense comfort and assurance from such a great and awesome God who could keep it all within His sovereign oversight and controlled limits. I rejoice that even the great needs of this day are no threat to Your omnipotent power and sovereign design.

I pray for a revolutionary revival to come from Your sovereign hand, and I affirm that Your omnipotence is sufficiently strong to bring it to pass. I affirm that Your omnipotent power is sufficient to humble the most hostile arrogance of man in a moment of time. I affirm that Your omnipotence is able to bring to nothing the most careful strategy and plan of Satan and his kingdom.

By faith I hold Your omniscient knowledge and Your total awareness in perspective as I pray. Thank You that there is no wickedness or sin that escapes Your knowledge. Thank You that the cross and redemptive work of our Lord Jesus Christ was sufficient to enable You to forgive the wickedness of man. I praise You that in Your omniscience You were able to apply His atoning blood to cleanse away the guilt of all my sins; none were missed. I hold Your omniscient understanding over the tragic conditions of the wicked rebellion of our age and ask You to humble us and bring us to repentance before You.

I worship You in the wonder of Your omnipresence. With the psalmist I acknowledge: "Where can I go from your Spirit? Where can I flee from your presence? If I go up to the heavens, you are there. If I make my bed in the depths you are there" (Psalm 139:7–8). Thank You that You are present wherever the dawn rises. In all of the extremities of space and in all of Your creation, You are there. Thank You that You inhabit eternity itself.

I rejoice that Your presence is as much with us in our day as it was there in the revival awakenings of history. I ask You to unveil Your presence among us. I invite You to draw near to us that we might experience the brokenness and the awareness of our sinful need that Your presence always brings. I affirm that revival comes as people become broadly aware of the near presence of our Holy God. I hold Your mercy and Your grace before You as providing sufficient ground for the fulfillment of this cry of my heart.

I exalt Your unchanging perfection in all that You are; You are the same yesterday, today, and forever. Thank You that Your promises are trustworthy. I believe that if Your people unite with You in the wonder of Your person and will seek Your face in humble prayer, You will hear us. I affirm my desire to turn from all my wicked ways and I cry out to You to hear from heaven, to forgive our sins, and to heal our land. In Your immutable, sovereign plan,

I look to You to effect all that is necessary to bring us to revival.

I exalt Your justice, Heavenly Father. I rejoice that You will one day banish all evil forever from Your presence in Your perfect plan of holy wrath. I also rejoice to see Your justice and truth displayed in loving mercy at Calvary. I acknowledge that Your holy wrath was requited by the atoning sacrifice of the Lord Jesus Christ. Thank You for being willing to place upon Your own Son the judgment that we, who have received Your grace instead, deserved. The wonder of that escapes my full capacity to understand. Yet, I know that Your justice, shown in such mercy and grace, remains at the very core of my prayer for revival. I ask for Your justice to draw near to us. I acknowledge that our culture deserves what came to Sodom and to the earth in Noah's day. I plead rather for the mercy and justice that came at Pentecost.

Thank You that many of those same people who had cried out for Christ to be crucified, cried out at Pentecost in broken repentance: "What shall we do? What shall we do?" Do it again, oh God. Judge us not with wrath as You did Sodom, but judge us with terrible conviction of sin until repentance flows down before You in great brokenness and rivers of tears.

You are wise and truthful, and faithful to Your Word of truth. I marvel and wonder after Your patient endurance with us. I acknowledge that I ask of You a hard thing. Thank You that You remain transcendent above all of the chaos upon this earth. I rejoice that, in the infinite greatness of Your highness and loftiness, You abide in the divine stillness of Your perfection.

I hunger and thirst for Your righteousness. I know it will necessitate a revolutionary revival for such righteousness to touch our culture in large degree, but in Your greatness, You can bring it to pass. As I worship You in Your greatness, I claim the Word of Your promise: "For this is what the high and exalted One says— he who lives forever, whose name is holy: 'I live in a high and holy place, but also with the one who is contrite and lowly in spirit, to

revive the spirit of the lowly and to revive the heart of the contrite'" (Isaiah 57:15). I ask that You would bring the truth of that
loving promise to reality in my life and in my culture. I affirm
that there is sufficient merit in the name and finished work of our
Lord Jesus Christ to accomplish even more than I ask or imagine.
It is in His name I pray. Amen.

REVIVAL PRAYER PATTERN 2: REPENTANCE AND INTERCESSION

Loving Heavenly Father, I come again to worship You in the
wonder of who You are. I approach You in the merit and worthiness of our Lord Jesus Christ. I open my whole being to the
controlling work of Your Holy Spirit. I invite Him to express His
interceding, His groaning, through my prayers in the ways that He
may choose. I yield to You, Heavenly Father, all of the faculties and
capacities You have placed within me to be used for Your glory. I
open my mind, will, and emotions to You so that You might share
with me Your burden for the church and for the lost around me.

I rejoice that my Lord Jesus Christ could weep over the
people of Jerusalem as they passed up His presence and His
caring love for them. Cleanse me of the coldness and indifference
that keeps me from shedding tears for the rebellious sin of today.
Share with me my Lord's tears. Allow me to feel the mourning
of Your Spirit's groaning for my broken world. Grant me Your
divine intervention to express within me a willingness to fast and
to spend time in extended sessions of prayer. Help me see those
times when I awaken in the night as opportunities to cry to You
for a revolutionary revival to visit Your church. What I pray for
myself I pray also for a large number of other believers whom You
are calling to a deeper prayer burden.

I confess my sins to you, dear Heavenly Father. Wash me
clean in my Savior's precious blood from all that offends You. I

recognize within my person a fleshly condition that can be rebellious in Your sight. Thank You for informing me of this fact in Your Word. I affirm that in my union with Christ in His death I am dead to the rule of that fleshly condition. I desire the new nature You effected within me to be in charge through the power of my Savior's resurrection. Thank You for having made this new creation in righteousness and true holiness, so I can love You deeply and serve You fully. May Your Holy Spirit enable me to manifest before You and others the fruit of His full control. In the name of the Lord Jesus Christ, I bind Satan and his host from interjecting any interference in my prayer.

I bring to You, Heavenly Father, the sins of my family, the church, and the culture in which I live. What great wickedness takes place in our homes. Thank You that it's not hidden from You. I repent of it for my family, other Christian families, and non-Christian families. You established the home, and it is very dear to You. Forgive us for the way we too often talk to each other in anger and unkindness. How broken You must be over the physical, verbal, and sexual abuse that is too much a part of the families in our culture. I not only confess this wickedness but I ask You to intervene and change it by Your mighty power. Show us our sins and grant us the grace of repentance. I recognize that the sins of our nation and culture are an abomination in Your eyes. I repent for our culture of the terrible abuse of our sexuality. The misuse of this God-given gift is a curse upon our times. I apologize to You, Heavenly Father, for the abomination of pornography and the wide audience that makes it profitable. Turn our hearts from this perversion. You intended that our sexual desires should glorify Your name within the sacred bonds of marriage. May this take place in our culture.

I repent before You, loving God, for the violence against innocent people that has invaded our culture. My heart grieves as Yours surely does for those multiplied millions of unborn babies that

have been destroyed by legalized abortions. I repent for our legislators and court judges, and for the people who let it go on. Forgive
and change the violence displayed in the entertainment media, in
the inner city, and in the drug scene. I apologize for the burgeoning
market for drugs and other intoxicants. My heart grieves for the
cursing and vile talk that streams forth from people's mouths.

I see spreading through our culture a plague of fascination
with the spirit realm of darkness. It poisons our little children in
the themes of their toys, games, and cartoons. It permeates our
entertainment media. It subtly is becoming a part of the business
and educational world through various trends and themes. A
growing host of people are so deceived that they are worshiping
Satan with animal and even human sacrifices. How terribly this
dishonors You, O Lord. I cry out against it in prayer and I repent
for them of this awful wickedness. I ask You to bring a revival
awakening so deep and intense that these things will be crushed
by Your almighty power.

Forgive us for all our wickedness, O God. The sin of our land
is so great. Religious sins of unbelief, legalism, and self-righteous
pride abound. Greed, covetousness, gluttony, gossip, and spiritual
indifference are almost as common to professing believers as to
the lost. We desperately need a holy revival from You to confront
our sins and bring us to humble repentance and spiritual renewal.

My hope, Heavenly Father, is in the promises of Your Word.
Thank You for Your compassion for us in our sinful ways. In our
arrogant lifestyle, we say to you, "I am rich. I have acquired wealth
and do not need a thing." I repent of that! I confess that, as believers, we show our wretched, pitiful, poor, blind, and naked condition. I accept that analysis by my Lord Jesus Christ as applying to
me and to my fellow believers.

Thank You that our Lord Jesus Christ has invited us to come
and buy from Him gold refined in His disciplining fires. I want
that gold for me and for Your church. I ask for the white clothes

that my Lord Jesus Christ promised would cover our nakedness. Anoint our eyes with the eye salve that enables us to see things as our Lord Jesus Christ sees them. I open the door of my life to my Lord Jesus Christ. I invite Him to come to me, to the church, and to our day to give us a mighty sense of His holy presence. May His nearness truly break us over our sins until we flee to the cross for cleansing by His blood. May this awakening for which I pray bring to saving faith multitudes who are not yet in our Savior's fold. Heavenly Father, move everything out of the way that hinders the coming of revival. Cause revival to affect churches, legislators, courts, businesses, education, government, and all that is before You. Will You not revive us again?

I lay all of this before You, Heavenly Father, basing every request on the merit and worthiness of our Lord Jesus Christ alone, and His finished work. I ask that You build a faith within me and countless numbers of other believers that is growing and contagious, and that rests totally upon Your will and plan for us in this day and upon the foundation of Your Word and the finished work of our Lord Jesus Christ. Amen.

REVIVAL PRAYER PATTERN 3: REVIVAL PRAYER GROUPS

Loving Heavenly Father, I worship You as the God who loves people. You have declared in Your Word that You are patient with people, not wanting anyone to perish—and You have provided opportunity for everyone to come to repentance. Thank You for Your patience that brought me to saving faith in the Lord Jesus Christ. I praise You, Heavenly Father, for demonstrating Your love by having the Lord Jesus Christ die for ungodly people while we were still in our sins. It is wonderful to know that You have loved humanity with such outreaching sacrifice that provides forgiveness and eternal life for all who believe. Thank You, Lord

Jesus Christ, for praying for those who believe in You. Thank You for the other sheep that You will one day bring to Yourself.

I pray with You, dear Savior, for those other sheep that You must bring. Multitudes are still bound by sin and Satan, and I ask forgiveness for myself and for other believers who have cared so little for those perishing people. I acknowledge that the same sinful culture that blinds and binds the lost has made my heart cold and apathetic. Please forgive me. Grant me a burden for the lost around me. I pray for [name persons you care for who are lost]. In the name of the Lord Jesus Christ, I tear down the blindness Satan is putting upon [name(s)]. Father, I pray You will bring these dear ones to saving faith in our Lord Jesus Christ.

Thank You, Father in heaven, for the revival awakenings of history. I praise You for giving revival blessings in various places, even in recent years. Thank You for opening my eyes to see the need for a revolutionary revival from Your omnipotent hands that will glorify You, startle the world, and bring multitudes to saving faith. I ask You to grant me a burden for such an awakening. Help me to believe that it can come to my city. I humbly offer myself as an intercessor for such an awakening. Lead me to at least one other person with whom I can pray regularly for coming revival. I ask You to raise up revival prayer groups in every city, town, suburb, and rural area of our nation. I ask You to build a broad base of people worldwide who are expecting revival. Grant to each group a consuming burden for You to bring revival. Make the involvement of people broad enough so that when You sovereignly know we are ready, You will visit us with Your holy presence. Your promise is that as we seek to draw near to You, You will draw near to us. I pray this nearness will truly be revolutionary. Make it humble us, break us, revive us, and change the direction of our disintegrating culture.

We desperately need a movement of Your mighty grace that will transform the lives of multitudes of people. Move our culture back to the absolutes of a Judeo-Christian ethic. Grant to us a legal system with courts that fear God and establish justice. Invade our penal system with such regeneration and reform that our jails will gradually empty until we wonder what to do with the unoccupied buildings.

I ask for such a transformation of our educational system that the humanistic, atheistic trends of our day will be completely reversed. I pray this revival will touch every political leader, every business enterprise, and every person in the mass media and entertainment industry. May revival clean up the music industry. I ask that the poverty, drunkenness, drugs, immorality, and violence so common in our inner cities be overwhelmed by the transformed lives of regenerated people who live there. Bring the pornography industry to its knees through the repentance of both the producers and consumers. Melt the divorce scandal away into nothingness because of the righteous, forgiving, encouraging lives of families made right with You.

The need for revolutionary revival in the churches, Lord Jesus Christ, is perhaps the greatest need of all. I invite You to walk among us who are professing believers and to expose our sins as You see them. Grant to Your church a thoroughly repentant spirit where jealousies, suspicions, and competitiveness evaporate in the abundance of joy that revival brings. I ask that every denomination and local church that honors You and proclaims Your Word will so overflow with people that petty differences will disappear and true worship that honors You will be established in the land. Enable the people to enjoy their preference of worship style in the fullness of Your Spirit.

Loving Heavenly Father, we are people with needs far greater than we understand. Come in the fullness and power of Your Holy Spirit and minister to us all. I open my life to You. Take every part of me and do with me whatever You know needs to be done. I hold back nothing from You. I believe there is sufficient grace supplied in the person and work of Jesus Christ to do far more than I have even begun to ask. I acknowledge that the Holy Spirit is mighty enough to humble the whole world with conviction of sin and the exalting of righteousness. I acknowledge, Almighty God, that You can quickly bring a world either to judgment or to revival. In the name of my Lord Jesus Christ, I plead for revolutionary revival to sweep over us like a fire that cannot be quenched. Amen.

REVIVAL PRAYER PATTERN 4: PROTECTION FROM THE ENEMY

Loving Heavenly Father, I worship you as the provider of my protection from the hurtful, murderous intent of my enemies. "See how numerous are my enemies and how fiercely they hate me" (Psalm 25:19). I desire not to passively assume my safety but to step deliberately with faith and understanding into that victory You have provided. Teach me how to appropriate my victory. I am listening for wise insights from You even as I address You in prayer. Teach me deeper love and understanding of Yourself, even as I open my whole person to You right now.

I plead that mighty name You have exalted above every name—Lord Jesus Christ—over my personal life and my walk with God; over my spouse, my children, and all for whom I am responsible in my family; over the ministry You have given to me and all for whom I am responsible in ministry. I uphold the name of my Lord Jesus Christ over Your church and all of Your will and plans for the bringing of revolutionary revival. I worship my Savior. I affirm that Jesus is Lord—Yahweh—and the more we know of Him, the more we know of You, Father. He is Jesus, Savior. He is my Savior; there is no Savior but Him. I worship Jesus as the One who took away my sins. He is the Christ—the Anointed of God. He is the anointed Prophet who proclaimed the way and who is the way. He is the anointed Priest who offers a better sacrifice for sin and is Himself that sacrifice. He is the anointed King who now rules in His sovereign power and who will one day rule as King of kings and Lord of lords.

I seek to abide in my Lord Jesus Christ and to hide in the protection of His almightiness and my oneness with Him. I abide in His incarnation, His humanity. How wonderful that You planned that our Savior should be one of us. The mystery of that remains beyond my capacities for understanding.

I abide in the surety that He experienced all of life's temptations and never once failed to meet sin's fullest challenge. He fulfilled all righteousness. He obeyed every particle of Your expectancy for us as expressed in Your Law. As one of us, He pleased You—His Heavenly Father—as a little child, as a youth, and as an adult in every aspect of His life.

Thank You that as one of us He completely overcame sin. In His humanity, He never yielded to sin's enticements, though He was made in "the likeness of sinful flesh." The world was never able to entice Him to accept its values or to press Him into its mold. Thank You that though Satan himself and his demons tried to cause Him to sin, in His humanity He willed not to sin. With joy I enter into His sinless, worthy human life and expect Your blessing because You have placed His worthiness upon me. There is safety and peace here, and I abide in it.

By faith, I abide in the sufferings and death of my Lord Jesus Christ. I claim the shelter of His precious blood over myself and those for whom I am responsible. It was in the work of His sufferings and death on the cross that You have removed the guilt of my sins. Cleanse me through His blood from all sins of omission and commission that would hinder my fellowship with You.

I abide in the sufferings and death of the Lord Jesus Christ who "destroyed him who had the power of death, that is the devil." I hold the victory of the cross against the devil and all of his kingdom. In the power of the sufferings and shed blood of my Savior, I resist all of Satan's efforts to harm me or those for whom I am responsible.

I affirm the mighty triumph of the Lord Jesus Christ in His resurrection from the dead. In the practical outliving of my life today, I desire to be clothed with that same mighty power that raised Jesus Christ from the dead. In His resurrection power, enable me to walk in newness of life. I address resurrection power directly against Satan and his kingdom in all his efforts to rule me and to hold back revival from coming to Christ's church.

By faith, I enter into the ascension of my Lord Jesus Christ, where He is seated far above all principalities and powers. Thank You, Heavenly Father, for raising me up with Christ and seating me with Him in the heavenly realms. Teach me more perfectly how to rest in the safety of that lofty position and how to use that authority to pull down all of Satan's ruling tactics.

I abide in my Savior's glorification. I submit to Your lordship over my life, my family, and Your church. I ask You to shepherd me in Your will and to hold me in the safety of Your faithful protection. I ask You to shepherd Your church to revival awakening in this day of great darkness.

Heavenly Father, I reach out for Your Holy Spirit and the wonder of His work. I rejoice that He came in fulfillment of the promise of both the Father and the Son. I rejoice that He convicted me and brought me to Christ, opened my eyes to see and caused me to be born of the Spirit. Thank You that He came to live within me the moment I was saved. I invite the Holy Spirit to enable me to walk in Him, so that love, joy, peace, patience, gentleness, goodness, meekness, faithfulness, and self-control may overflow from my life. May others see this, especially those close to me. May I see His fruit, but most of all, may His control be evident to You, O Lord.

I abide in His sealing, protecting work. I abide in His having made me a member of Christ's body. Help me to minister to the body of Christ today. I depend upon Him to breathe His quickening life and power into me. May the Holy Spirit pray through me and may He endue me with His power to witness of You before others. I pray the mighty work of the Holy Spirit as God's "holy finger" directly against Satan and his kingdom. May the mighty power of the Holy Spirit confront and defeat the devil in all of his hurtful designs for this day. I ask the Holy Spirit to increase His powerful work of convincing our world of sin, of righteousness, and of judgment to come.

By faith I reach out for the wholeness of Your armor, Heavenly Father. I receive the belt of truth and by faith I wear it. Help me not to deceive or be deceived in any way.

I wear the breastplate of righteousness. Having none of my own righteousness, I desire to walk in the adequate supply of Your righteousness.

Help me to walk in my shoes of peace. I claim my peace with God through justification, my peace of God through prayer and the Spirit's work, and the near presence of the God of peace who is able to make even my enemies to be at peace with me.

Be my shield today, dear Lord. May Your presence hedge me in and quench all of Satan's flaming arrows.

Helmet my head with Your salvation. May the Savior cover my mind to protect me from Satan's intruding thoughts. May the Lord Jesus Christ think His thoughts in my mind today.

I receive the Word of God as the Spirit's sword. Teach me to use it proficiently in my protection and in my witness. Help me to memorize it and to know its power.

I thank You, Heavenly Father, that my victory in Christ is not merely protective. You have provided me safety, so that I might be bold to address my Lord's victory against everything that opposes Your will. In the name of my Lord Jesus Christ, I tear down all that Satan has strategized to hinder revival awakening. I invite my living Lord Jesus Christ to sovereignly shepherd and lead His church into all that is necessary to bring revival. I invite the Holy Spirit to sovereignly move to prepare the people whom You have chosen to be leaders in each phase of revival preparation. I invite the Holy Spirit to prepare those special servants through whom God's call for revival will come.

I give myself to You, loving God and Father of our Lord Jesus Christ. In the worthiness of my Lord, and in the enablement of Your Holy Spirit, I offer myself to You for any purpose You may have. Through Jesus Christ my Lord, I pray. Amen.

REVIVAL PRAYER PATTERN 5: COMING AGAINST THE ENEMY

Loving Heavenly Father, You are the stronghold of my life; of whom shall I be afraid? I worship You and love You for being omnipotent, almighty, and absolute in Your transcendent greatness and unequaled power. Thank You that no matter how formidable and threatening the forces of darkness become, those who are with us are always "more" than those who are with them. I affirm that Your almightiness is unapproachable by any challenger and that Your power is full of glory.

I worship You, Heavenly Father, in the worthy merit of the Lord Jesus Christ. I affirm that He is Lord to the glory of God the Father. I hold all of His person and work directly upon my life as my protection during this time of prayer. I choose to abide in His incarnation, His cross, His resurrection, His ascension, and His glorification.

I come in humble obedience to use the weapons of my warfare against the darkness that is seeking to rule the people of my city, country, and world. I affirm that the weapons You have given to me to use are filled with divine power that is sufficient to demolish every stronghold Satan has built in attempts to thwart Your will and plan.

I confess the awful wickedness and sins that I, my family, my fellow believers, and my culture have committed. Wash me afresh in the blood of my Lord Jesus Christ, that there may be no hindrance to Your fellowship and blessing upon me. I apologize to You for the offense against You represented in the wicked sins characterizing our culture. I recognize that when people abandon themselves in such sinful rebellion, much ground is being given to Satan to rule in our culture. My one hope is in knowing that the finished work of my Lord Jesus Christ is sufficient payment for even these. I ask You to bring about all that is necessary to grant us the gift of repentance and a broken humility before You. I invite You to draw near to the people of our day until we are humbled and broken before You in a spiritual awakening greater than any that has ever been.

In the mighty name of my Lord Jesus Christ, I use the weapons of my warfare to demolish and weaken every throne, dominion, princely ruler, authority, power of darkness, and wicked spirit in the heavenly realm that is organized and strategized to hinder revival. I ask the Holy Spirit to hold the mighty power of the shed blood and finished work of my Lord Jesus Christ constantly against these strongholds to cause their destruction and defeat.

In the name of the Lord Jesus Christ and by the power of His blood, I pull down all levels of the stronghold of [choose items from the following list of areas of Satan's strongholds that God leads you to pull down and smash; you may think of other things, for the list is suggestive, not exhaustive].

1. Pornography
2. Perverted sexual practices
3. Adultery and prostitution
4. Drug use and promotion

5. Drug suppliers' protection
6. Alcohol addiction
7. Abortion practices and promotion
8. Cursing and vile language
9. Unbelief and humanism
10. New Age teaching
11. Occult promotion and activity
12. Satan worship
13. Television and media distortions
14. Religious cults and -isms (name those you know)
15. Promotion of liberal theology and false teaching
16. Divisive influences in the body of Christ
17. Violence and crime
18. Racism
19. Child abuse in all its forms
20. Divorce and family disunity
21. Materialism and greed
22. Evil peer pressure
23. Spiritual deafness and spiritual blindness
24. Blocking of people from sharing their faith
25. Blocking of people from receiving Christ
26. Lack of care for the homeless and hurting
27. Disunity and distrust in Christ's Body
28. Attacks on pastors, Christian workers, and their families
29. Interest in spiritism and evil supernaturalism
30. Promotion of hate, rage, and violent anger
31. Hindrance of the recruitment and funding of missionaries
32. Pride, spiritual haughtiness, and indifference
33. Neglect of Bible study and prayer
34. Disbelief in the spiritual consequences of sin
35. Disbelief in the work and schemes of the devil
36. Disbelief in the command to personally resist the devil

I pull down these strongholds in the name of my Lord Jesus Christ and I pray their wicked work back upon themselves. I ask my loving Father in heaven to assign His holy angels to engage in direct combative defeat of these strongholds of evil. I bind the work of evil powers in each of these strongholds and I invite the Holy Spirit to unleash His mighty convicting power upon the people who are in bondage to them. I ask Him to exalt the ways of righteousness before the spiritual understanding of such people and to convict them deeply of their accountability to God in coming judgment. I ask the Holy Spirit to open their spiritual eyes to see their need for the saving grace of our Lord Jesus Christ. May this revival for which I pray bring multitudes into a saving relationship with Him.

I address my prayer against the strongholds assigned to keep God's people from believing You for revival awakening. Surely, there must be many that are working to make Your people luke-warm, satisfied with our materialism, and blind to our spiritual needs. I pull down all such strongholds, named and unnamed, and I pray for a great moving of the Holy Spirit to bring to us a hungering and a thirsting after righteousness. May the Holy Spirit produce in Christ's Body an insatiable appetite to memorize, study, and know God's Holy Word. In the name of my Lord Jesus Christ I plead for a revolutionary revival to visit my heart, my family, my church, and the whole body of Christ until it spills over into the world around us and brings many souls into glory. Amen.

REVIVAL PRAYER PATTERN 6: UNITY IN THE BODY

Dear God and Father of our Lord Jesus Christ, I worship You in the wonder of Your triune oneness. I grope to understand the mystery of how three unique persons remain one God. I praise

You for its truth and I bow before You in the wonder of such revelation of Yourself. By faith, I ask You to increase my capacity to appreciate and understand Your triune oneness that I might share new insights with others.

I also praise and worship You, Lord Jesus Christ, for the scope of Your finished work that unites me with You. I hold Your powerful name, Lord Jesus Christ, over my personal life, my family, my work, and the whole body of Christ for benefit, protection, and all that You have for us.

I rejoice that Your salvation has united me inseparably not only with Yourself but also with every other born-again believer. Thank You, blessed Holy Spirit, for Your great work of baptizing me into this body of Christ. I rejoice to be a part of such perfect fellowship. Thank You, Lord Jesus Christ, for continuing Your mighty work of readying Your body to present her to Yourself as a radiant church, without stain, wrinkle, or blemish of any kind. Thank You that this body will be holy and blameless in the mystery of Your finished work. I glory in the wonder of such truth.

I enter into repentance and confession before You to acknowledge how often I personally have violated the essential oneness of the body. Cleanse me of my wickedness of not honoring each part of the body as You do. I also confess the sins of my family and fellow church members in not living out the unity of the body which You have created. I confess the divisiveness existing in Your visible church as a violation of Your holy plan. I worship and praise You, dear Heavenly Father, for Your sovereign ability to use even our divisiveness to glorify Your name and finish Your work.

Yet I long and pray for the bringing together of Your born-again ones in a united movement for revival awakening. We have been so deeply wounded by those things that have divided us. Our capacity to bring about change in our world has been reduced to a feeble squeak. In humble embarrassment I repent

221

over this fact and ask Your Holy Spirit to move over Your body to cause change. Help us to come together under the oneness of the Holy Spirit's control. May the oneness of intercession wait before heaven's throne of grace in the hearts of millions of believers who are asking God for revolutionary revival.

Thank You, Lord Jesus Christ, for planning for unity rather than uniformity. The diversity of Your body is part of its beauty and functional appeal to the lost. It testifies to Your glory. Bless Your church in its wide diversity of expression in patterns of worship and songs of praise. Help us to love one another in our diversity.

Help me not to condemn my fellow members for what they are not. Grant me the wisdom to understand and the capacity to appreciate them for who they are. Above all, help me to love each part of the body. May that love express itself in patience and the capacity to hold my thoughts in check when I see the failures of another member of Your body. Forgive me for my quick practice to take comfort about my own failures when I see the sins of others.

Blessed Heavenly Father, I recognize that Satan and his kingdom are relentless in their efforts to keep believers divisive toward one another. As the accuser of the believers, he continually plants suspicions in believers' hearts. In the name of my Lord Jesus Christ, I pull down that wicked work of darkness and bind our enemy so that he may not succeed. I ask the Holy Spirit to supplant all divisive works with the unity of the Spirit actively working in believers.

Oh, Holy God, only Your sovereignty can move Your body into united action. May Your Holy Spirit brood over Your church and cause it to breathe out a united cry for revival awakening. I wait before You for this. Only You can work it out in a way that will startle the world and glorify Your name. Raise up the leaders You can trust to touch not the glory that belongs only to You. I affirm again that what You have accomplished through the finished work of my Lord Jesus Christ is sufficient to do more than I ask. In Jesus' precious name I pray. Amen.

REVIVAL PRAYER PATTERN 7: THE WORD OF GOD

Loving Heavenly Father, I come to worship You in the wonder of what You have chosen to reveal in Your Word about Yourself. The majesty of Your creation displays Your awesome greatness. I see Your omnipotence when I look upon the vastness of the universe. I praise You that You are everywhere, present in all the extremities of the universe, and that You are greater than Your creation.

I look upon the immensity of man's accumulated knowledge and remember Your omniscient possession of all knowledge. The steady march of time causes me to reflect upon the fact that You are eternal, without beginning or end. The lying, sinful ways of humanity evident everywhere cause me to long for the one who is Truth and who reigns in absolute justice.

I praise You, loving God and Father of our Lord Jesus Christ, for what You have revealed about Yourself in the written Word of God. I affirm that Your Holy Word is an inerrant revelation of Your holy Truth. I ask forgiveness for my neglect in reading, memorizing, and meditating upon Your Word. What an ugly, sinful wrong it is for me, my family, and my fellow believers to treat Your holy Word so lightly when it has been made so available to us. Wash away our guilt and create within our hearts a longing to know and read Your Word.

Through Your Word, Heavenly Father, I came to know the Lord Jesus Christ as my Savior from sin. In Your Word He is revealed as the One who became God in human flesh and was victorious in Himself over the world, the flesh, and the devil. In Your

Word I learn that though He was tempted in every way that I am tempted, He never sinned. Your Word declares that, as one of us, He fulfilled all righteousness. Your Word declares that He was wounded for my transgressions and bruised for my iniquities. It declares that He became sin for me and that my sins and offenses against You were laid upon Him when He died in my place upon the cross.

It is in Your Word that the mighty truth of His triumph over death and the grave in resurrection power is established. Your Word declares with assuring detail the Lord Jesus Christ's ascension into heaven and His present glorified overseeing of His church. Because of the declarations of Your Word, I look for my Savior to come again with power and great glory. I love You, Heavenly Father, for having given me Your Word.

I praise You, loving God, that You have graced us with the coming of the Holy Spirit at Pentecost. Thank You for revealing Your Word to me in the wonder of His mighty work in this world and in believers. Thank You for declaring in Your Word that the Holy Spirit came to convict the world of its sin and guilt. I ask for the Holy Spirit to greatly intensify His work of convincing people of their sin against a holy God. May the Holy Spirit so open people to the spiritual seeing and hearing of Your Word that they again will cry out in repentance. Thank You also that the Holy Spirit exalts righteousness by revealing the righteous things of Your Word. I ask Him to do that with powerful persuasion.

I pray that the Holy Spirit will, by Your Word, reveal to human hearts the certainty of an approaching accountability to God. May that sobering fact settle upon people until they can find no rest apart from coming to our Lord Jesus Christ.

Blessed Holy Spirit, You are the one who breathed out God's Word in divine revelation through human instruments. I ask You now to use that Word to speak personally to believers. Grant new insights to God's appointed leaders to promote reading, memorizing, and meditating upon God's Word among God's people. I ask You, Holy Spirit, to raise up anointed revivalists, evangelists, and preachers who will be able to make the Bible known with compelling power to a lost world.

I pray the mighty power of God's holy Word against Satan and his kingdom. Confront and defeat Satan's lies with the truth of Your Word. May the comfort of Your Word relieve people from Satan's accusations, torments, and terror. I ask that the warnings of Your Word will alert people to Satan's tactics to bring them into bondage. Invade Satan's kingdom with salvation's message in Your Word, and bring multitudes from the darkness of hell into the kingdom of light and eternal life.

I recognize, Heavenly Father, that revival will never come unless a deep, personalized hearing of Your Word comes to human hearts. In the name of my Lord Jesus Christ and by the power of His blood, I pull down Satan's power to dishonor and discredit God's holy Word. In prayer I apply the power of the Holy Spirit against all satanic strongholds assigned to hinder the Word of God from being heard and understood by the hearts of people. I invite the blessed Holy Spirit to exalt the Word of God and to reveal its mighty power in ways that will confound the enemies of truth. Cause people to hear Your Word with a new, profound depth, and move pastors and churches to proclaim and teach Your Word with a contagious freshness.

I affirm, Heavenly Father, that Your Word is alive and powerful. I rejoice that though heaven and earth will pass away, not one tiny word of your holy truth will ever fall. Grant Your Word great success in our day. Use Your holy Word to move our nation to revolutionary revival. I love Your Word, O Lord, and I give myself to know it better and to live it out more. I offer this prayer in the name of Him who is the Living Word, my Lord Jesus Christ. Amen.

DEEPER WALK INTERNATIONAL

D eeper Walk International, Inc. was originally organized and known as the International Center for Biblical Counseling (ICBC). Since its inception, this ministry has sought to provide biblically balanced teaching and guidance for helping spiritually oppressed individuals. Our goal includes the desire to provide an international forum among Christian professionals, ministers, missionaries, and laypeople on the subject of helping the spiritually needy. Christian disciples need to learn and practice a biblical worldview that provides stability and a spiritual walk of freedom.

While still serving as a pastor, Dr. Mark Bubeck helped found ICBC and served as its president before retiring. His book *The Adversary* was first published in 1975 and is still widely used to provide a foundational understanding of the spiritual battles of life. He has written four other books that have contributed helpful study to the believer's dealings with the world, the flesh, and the devil. His strong advocacy for "doctrinal prayer" is set forth in all of his writings and is expressed in numerous written prayers. *Prayer Patterns for Revival* presents seven doctrinal prayers designed for a believer's daily intercessions for revival.

Dr. Bubeck still serves as president emeritus of Deeper Walk International. He strongly supports the leadership of Dr. Marcus Warner, the current president of Deeper Walk International. Dr. Warner brings a passion for heart-focused discipleship and for expanding the number of workers around the world who are able to assist the hurting.

Deeper Walk International provides training and resources that are designed to assist and better equip Christian leaders to counsel those in spiritual bondage. In every way that our experience and assets permit, Deeper Walk International will encourage other organizations and geographic centers in the establishment of similar ministries that reach out to hurting, oppressed souls.

Deeper Walk International is a nonprofit, tax-exempt corporation functioning on a donation basis. The gifts of those who have a vital interest in this ministry as well as those who have benefited from it provide the financial base needed to support this work.

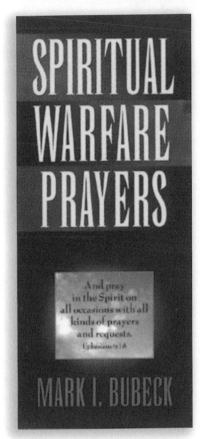

978-0-8024-7132-1

In this handy pamphlet, sized to slide into your Bible or notebook and perfect for use in churches or small groups, Mark Bubeck offers twenty prayers, rich in doctrine, to help Christians triumph in their spiritual battles. Model prayers include those for:

- Revival
- Repentance
- Intercession
- Protection from the Enemy
- Unity in the Body
- Wearing the Armor of God

Learn to pray like the disciples did—by example.

Also available as an ebook

MOODY
Publishers

From the Word to Life

From Mark I. Bubeck

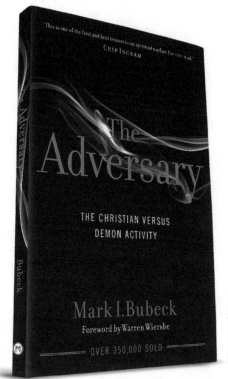

978-0-8024-0991-1

In this classic bestseller, Bubeck offers a mature, biblical perspective on dealing with the devil and demonic powers. With over 350,000 copies sold, these clear explanations have helped thousands of Christians recognize their victory in the spiritual realm.

Also available as an ebook

MOODY
Publishers®

From the Word to Life®

CONSIDER THIS BOOT CAMP FOR SPIRITUAL WARFARE.

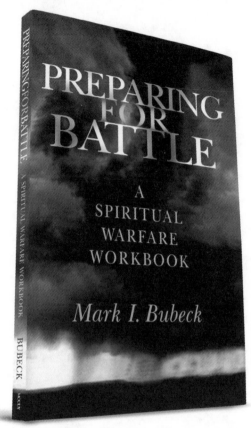

978-0-8024-9082-7

Unfortunately, many of us do little to strengthen ourselves when it comes to the area of spiritual warfare. As a result, the forces of hell have a heyday messing with our lives. We wonder why our lives are in such turmoil instead of realizing how unprepared we are. In *Preparing for Battle*, each thought-provoking lesson contains:

- A Scripture text for meditation
- An opening prayer
- A variety of questions to discuss and answer
- Insights on how to spiritually equip yourself

Also available as an ebook

MOODY
Publishers®

*From the Word **to** Life®*

MOODY Radio™

*From the Word **to Life***

Moody Radio produces and delivers compelling programs filled with biblical insights and creative expressions of faith that help you take the next step in your relationship with Christ.

You can hear Moody Radio on 36 stations and more than 1,500 radio outlets across the U.S. and Canada. Or listen on your smartphone with the Moody Radio app!

www.moodyradio.org